TRAJECTORY

Your Personal Flightpath of Purpose

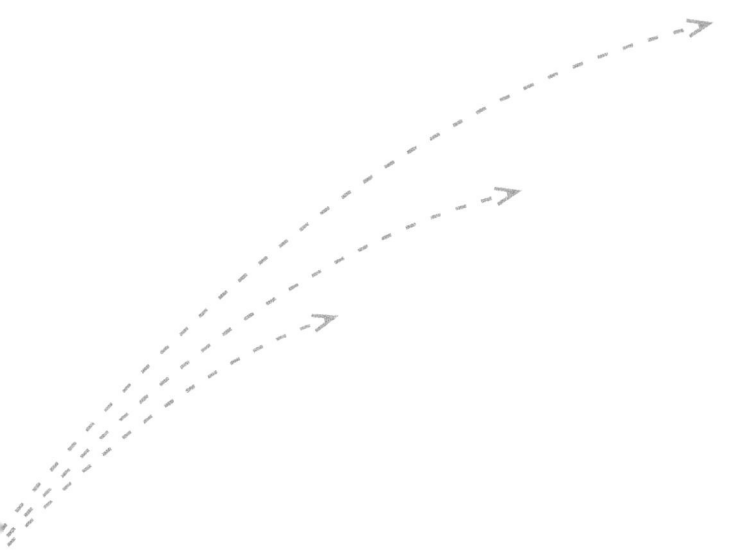

STEVEN BOLT

Copyright © 2018 Steven Bolt

All rights reserved. No part of this publication may be reproduced, distributed, or transmitted in any form or by any means, including photocopying, recording, or other electronic or mechanical methods, without the prior written permission of the publisher, except for the personal use of the product purchaser.

This book is dedicated to:

My beautiful wife, Vicky Bolt, who has been my constant companion for the largest part of my personal trajectory, and what a loving, encouraging, and fun companion she is!

I also want to dedicate this collection of words to those who want a "more" kind of life, and are prepared to stay the course to see it.

Thanks are also due to those who have personally inspired me to pursue purpose and see beyond the now.

Contents

1 Introduction

5 Stargazing—A Vision for Your Life

13 The Laboratory—Planning

45 Launch—Getting Started

73 Trajectory—Your Personal Flightpath

91 Mission Destination

103 Mission Debrief

117 Notes

121 About the Author

Introduction

I was talking to a mate recently about where he was headed and some of his recent history. The word "trajectory" came to mind as we thought about the many variables that go into shaping our life course, our personal trajectory.

It seemed that "trajectory" was a word from God in the moment to help encourage and bring perspective for this particular individual. My comment to him however, was that it felt like there was some more downloading to come. In other words, stay tuned!

In the weeks that followed, I found myself listening to others, continually thinking, "Oh, you're describing an aspect of your trajectory," and I began to wonder if God might be downloading some wisdom and encouragement for more than one individual. The word became a multifaceted image swirling inside my mind. I had the bright idea to represent it in a painting. Then I remembered I can barely draw, let alone paint!

To top things off, other people started using the word "trajectory" in conversation. Now that, I thought, is unusual!

After a few more weeks, (evidence of how dim I can be at times), the thought occurred to me that this was a word ripe for a wider audience than I had first thought. This was followed by being awakened from my sleep with the instruction, "This is a book, write it quickly". So here we are.

Merriam Webster's Collegiate Dictionary (Eleventh Edition) defines trajectory in the first instance as:

"The curve that a body (as a planet or comet in its orbit or a rocket) describes in space"

And just for good measure, here are some synonyms:

Course, route, path, track, flight, flightpath, direction

For some reason, the "rocket trajectory" definition especially resonates with me. Perhaps it has to do with a childhood memory I have of praying for the stricken Apollo 13 spacecraft to return safely to Earth.

It is the rocket trajectory definition set in the context of an overall space mission that I will use to highlight some key landmarks, stages, and cautions for our diverse life journeys.

Throughout the book I will refer to quotes from astronauts about their experiences. For example: *"It feels like someone's revealing a secret to you. Like you're getting to see something magic for the first time. It feels like an honour. Like a huge privilege."*

This is astronaut Chris Hadfield's response to being asked how it feels to see the earth from space for the first time.

The truth is that there are magnificent secrets waiting to be revealed to and through us as we follow our intended course on the way to achieving our individual missions. There are unique and wonderful perspectives that will be realized only as we summit the next objective along the way. And it is an honor more than it is a duty. It is a privilege to have the opportunity to live lives of significance and influence.

Our sphere of operation may not be as visually spectacular as hurtling through space in a tin can, but it can be every bit as spectacular in terms of your eternal achievement and the kingdom perspectives gained, as we behold God up close and personal.

The purpose of this book is to remind us to live deliberately toward kingdom objectives. The purpose of this book is to point to purpose.

Maybe you have never considered that your life has significant purpose. Maybe within your own thoughts you have flirted with the idea that there might be more to your life than you've currently experienced. Perhaps you have let go of a pursuit of purpose because something or someone strangled the life out of your hope. Perhaps you feel like you are well on course to purposeful living.

Whoever you are and wherever you see your life currently, there are encouragement and direction in these pages.

My personal experience has been a bumpy ride with mixed reviews. My trajectory thus far has been an odd combination of deep valleys, incredible highs, and some extended times that have felt completely dead, or at the very least, dormant.

God has been there the whole time, working the plan that He created for me before I was born. Many times, I've forgotten that fact. Many times, I have underestimated both myself and God. That is a terrible confession, but it is a true one.

At times God has been calling from way out in front of me. Sometimes His voice can be heard over my shoulder as He directs me from a location somewhere behind me. At other times, I am fully aware of His presence; we are walking side by side and there is no distance or misunderstanding between us.

There have been still other times where I have been so focused on the current circumstance or crisis that His voice has seemed silent.

This book is meant to encourage you, wherever you are on your journey, by reminding you that whatever the prevailing conditions in your life right now, they are temporary. A snapshot of your "now" moment may be grim, but it is just a fraction of your lifetime journey. My hope is that this book will help us all to broaden our perspective.

If you are in a place of plenty, don't get so comfortable that you forget your purpose. If you are in a place of difficulty, hang on, you can outlast it.

All the highs, the lows, the wins, and the fails are shaping you and propelling you along your trajectory toward your unique purpose.

So, let's *launch* right into it!

Stargazing – A Vision for Your Life

There are probably not too many of us who have looked up at the star strewn night sky without a sense of awe, and wondered at the scale and content of it all. Authors down through the ages have told many a story, imagining what lies beyond our understanding and reach. Lovers have recounted their love for each other by the silvery light of the moon and the cascades of galactic clusters. Scientists have sought to know and to understand our own origins by looking outward and upward.

Whether it is an ancient shepherd reclining alongside his flocks at night, or an astrophysicist pushing out the realms of knowledge to discover and explain how the universe works, there is something in man that wants to look for more, that wants to look beyond what we have thus far experienced and known.

It's that kind of drive (and some healthy Cold War competitiveness) that drove the frenetic pace of the space race between USSR and USA, starting in the 1950s and lasting for roughly two decades.

It's that same kind of drive that still fuels the search for places to go in space, how to get there faster, and how to make sense of what we find.

It's a drive that propels modern day endeavors to inhabit Mars!

It's that kind of drive that mirrors our creator. From His eternal vantage point, He takes in all of time and all of space in every detail. In fact, He sustains it! Made in His likeness, we inherently seek to discover what He already knows, and we seek to discover the particular course our lives are meant to take. What is our personal trajectory?

In our relationship with Him we seek to progress along the trajectory that He has carefully mapped out for us in our appointed time.

As His children, God has put in our hearts the capacity to develop vision for what we cannot yet see, understand, or experience.

Our individual futures present opportunity to partner together with God, in traversing the expanse of time allotted to each of us, to not only a destination of purpose, but a unique journey of purpose.

Our Father in heaven who knows our beginning from our end, is willing to share direction for our individualized missions with those who will trust Him and who will remain obedient in the moment, though our course ahead and its purpose remain obscured.

The naked eye can be trained to recognize the familiar star formations in the night sky and can even track the reflected light of a satellite orbiting overhead. A conventional telescope can peer across vast distances to pinpoint a celestial body with laser accuracy. A radio telescope that combines a collection of radio dishes arrayed over large areas can be tuned to pick up the most remote and faint radio waves from outer space.

Likewise, the human spirit can be trained to detect the tiniest details and signals from our surrounds, to discover and begin to progress along the correct trajectory.

Every space mission begins with someone looking up and knowing that there is more. From the knowing comes the decision to go and find it, and from the decision comes the mapping of the pathway toward the desired vision, and the identifying and utilizing of the resources to get there.

Our own lives mimic the space mission scenario when we allow God to lead us to a grander vision and purpose for our lives than we can imagine on our own. It continues as we attune ourselves to Him and the directions He gives us through His voice, circumstance, and the counsel of others; the unique way in which we are designed and wired and by matching the desires of our own hearts with His.

Here is a quick note on becoming attuned to our Father's voice: There are many good undertakings and an abundance of sound advice directing us in improving our ability to hear God, but for me there is one that is better than the rest, and that is reading scripture.

Rom 10:17 says:

"So then, Faith comes by hearing, and hearing by the word of God."

Faith expects trusts and acts. Faith expects that our Father has a purpose and a specific trajectory for us and trusts Him to be on the journey with us. That faith then causes us to act in obedience and stay on the course.

This kind of faith comes from hearing God and according to our scripture, the ability to hear God comes from his word. How can we accurately read indicators around us or trust our inner thoughts if we don't first recognize His voice?

You know, it was over thirty years ago when I sat on a rickety old bus at a bus stop on Military Rd, Cremorne in Sydney. The building in front of the bus stop was a mix of office space and retail. Downstairs was a trendy little piano wine bar. (It was the 1980s and wine bars were popular. I went there once with a group of friends who were much more refined than I. I never understood why they insisted on me tagging along with them. I suspect they saw me as a goodwill project. God bless them.)

It was early morning. I was a 22-year-old apprentice mechanic on my way to work and had given my heart to Christ some months before. I was reading the bible and I sensed God speak to me for the very first time. The surprise was breathtaking. The excitement was electric. Over 30 years have passed and as you can see, it was a moment of such significance that all of the surrounding detail is etched into my memory.

Our personal trajectory begins when we realize that we have a unique and purposeful life to live, and that God has gazed into it and has been speaking into it since before we were born.

Vision for the *Trajectory* Book

Allow me to lay out the life cycle of this book as an illustration for each phase of our own mission cycle and trajectory.

I've already mentioned how the idea for this book came out of a number of conversations with others and with God. Those conversations brought into sharp focus a vision to take the trajectory message and present it in a book format. The vision was vague and undefined at first. In reality, I underestimated and misunderstood it at the outset. Applied time in thought and prayer helped the vision to shift from an idea out there, to a living idea inside of me.

What you wouldn't know is my longstanding vision to write. At around eight years old, I read my first book. The title was "Man Overboard" and I don't recall the story at all. What I do recall was the sensation of being transported into an adventure as I lie in my bed and read. I found myself injected as a hero into a story line that bore no resemblance to my reality.

The experience made me want to write and so began my quest. You know how sometimes an inspiring idea gets a hold of you and you do something stupid because…well, just because?

The copy of "Man Overboard" I had was very old and the pages were yellowed with age. Achieving this look for my pages was the starting point for an authentic adventure story, I was certain. So I proceeded to trial "aging" some blank pages of my writing paper. With my mum's protests of setting her kitchen on fire somewhere in the background of my consciousness, I waited patiently at the door of the oven as each attempt to create my book worthy paper failed.

Eventually I moved on from that project to something else that I'm sure seemed so important at the time, and the vision to write a book faded.

About a decade ago, during the annual goal setting session my wife and I do together, the vision resurfaced and I tentatively wrote a note to write a book at some unspecified point in the future. The commitment level was pretty low, but this is now my second foray into producing a published work and the vision is surely alive.

Stargazing Checklist

1. When do you most experience God's presence, power and pleasure? *(Who are you with, what are you doing, where are you?)*

2. How do you most sense God's direction? *(Pictures, words, phrases, scriptures, inner voice, from prevailing circumstance, activity)*

3. When do you feel most energized?

4. Where do you feel the greatest sense of challenge or even failure?

5. Where do you see the most fruit for effort in your life?

6. What do others say about you? *(If you're not sure, ask a few people who know you well enough to answer accurately and mature enough to answer honestly **and** lovingly)*

7. If you have a spouse, what do they say about you and what are the complimentary or joint trajectories that you each have?

8. What area of your life do you sense the most ease, the most peace?

9. What things make you most angry?

10. Looking at your answers to the questions so far, is there a pattern? Is there a recurring theme? Is there something that you identify as being most likely on the heart of God for you?

11. Is there just one thing that you could not bear to think about leaving this life without achieving, improving, influencing, initiating or contributing to?

12. Are there any crazy ideas from your past that maybe aren't as dead as you might think?

13. What has God been saying to you as you read this chapter?

14. Ask God to help you identify and prioritize what is really important for you to see as your future. Ask His help to see more and to hear His voice more clearly.

Inevitably through life we are drawn to look upward and outward. Like our Father in heaven we are creative creatures of power and vision and it is in us to reach for what is yet beyond our reach.

Depending on the intended purpose for a spacecraft, and the vision that mapped out its trajectory, an individual craft may pass a number of significant milestones and achieve a number of complementary and opportune missions along its flightpath. Our father did not make us as one trick ponies. While we are likely to have a main purpose for our course in life, that course, that trajectory is likely to have multifaceted, complementary purposes along the way that can arrive at seemingly random times. But random they are not.

The Laboratory— Planning

After developing a sense of purpose and destination which is normally an ongoing process with some light bulb moments along the way, we are faced with the enormous task of figuring out what is required to get there and in which direction do we start.

Finding my way around Sydney, pre-Google maps, was somewhat of a challenge for a Perth boy when I arrived in the early 1980s. Often times it felt like to get to a particular place across the city, the best course to take was one headed in roughly the opposite direction.

Sometimes the right plan for your purpose will seem so counterintuitive that it must be wrong. Kind of like Sydney without Google maps.

If you check out the link (https://airandspace.si.edu/multimedia-gallery/5317hjpg?id=5317), you will see an image of the planned trajectory for the Apollo 11 Mission. You'll notice that after liftoff the craft heads around the back of the earth, away from the planned mission to the moon. The right trajectory, to the untrained eye, would have seemed to be the completely wrong trajectory, and doesn't it look that way sometimes in our own lives?

Trust God

Astronauts on those missions and indeed on any mission must have absolute trust in their mathematicians, scientists, engineers, and all who make the journey possible. We must have absolute trust in Christ who is the author of our mission. The good news is we can have complete trust in not only his capacity but his intention. Both are perfect.

Someone, in fact a team of teams when it comes to a space mission, dedicate themselves to foolproof, failsafe planning to get the job done. Someone, your Father in heaven, has dedicated himself to your purposeful trajectory and he never makes a mistake.

Think about the first planned flight to the moon within the constraints of the technology and capacity of the time (late 1960s to early '70s). Think about all the requirements that had to be met; propulsion, guidance, communication, life support, structural integrity of craft, and probably a thousand other systems. Consider that successfully bringing all that together is not done in isolation. It has to be achieved in real time with an incredibly delicate operation of balancing all of the forces at work inside and outside of the craft, through every moment of the journey. Gravity, thrust, pressure, temperature, atmosphere, etc.

Follow this link to see a wall chart of the process flow for a NASA project/Program. Check out the detail in it, and then remember that this chart is just a very brief overview of some of the main details of a mission or project. Then consider that the detail and forethought that is involved in getting you to successfully complete your mission makes this look simple. Isn't it a great comfort to know we have the perfect mission oversight in relationship with God?

Plans and back up plans for every conceivable scenario are created, and it should come as no surprise to us that God has every detail, and every variable for our mission covered when he plots our trajectory and equips us for the journey.

Ephesians 2:10 says it this way:

"For we are His workmanship, created in Christ Jesus for good works, which God prepared beforehand, that we would walk in them."

Space mission scientists and engineers create a mission plan, including mission specific trajectory with the expectation that the craft will function as designed and travel exactly along the intended route, despite having external forces applied to it that can push the craft off course and into oblivion.

Similarly, our Father has perfectly planned our individual and mission specific trajectories, taking into account every force acting in, on, and around us. I've heard Dr. Lance Walnau say this, "God has already factored your incompetence into your destiny." Isn't that encouraging?

Delving into an arena that has formally been beyond our knowledge and capacity mean it is quite possible for mission planners to overlook, misunderstand, or simply not imagine a factor that has never been witnessed before.

It's good to know that mistakes and oversights are not a consideration when our perfect Father has planned our trajectory. Not only does He have every detail covered, the verse above reminds us that he has had it covered since before we even set foot on this earthly life.

This truth is vital to remember when we might consider giving up or aborting our mission. This is never truer than when it is us who have brought about the apparent failure situation by our own doing. When this is the case, the temptation is to throw our hands up and walk away thinking that we have blown it; that the master mission planner cannot recover the situation and wouldn't trust us to continue it, even if he could.

Remember Dr. Lance Walnau's words, and remember these words from Romans 3: 23-26:

> "...for all have sinned and fallen short of the glory of God, being justified freely by His grace through the redemption that is in Christ Jesus,...to demonstrate at the present time His righteousness, that He might be just, and be the justifier of the one who has faith in Christ Jesus."

There is not one among us whom God has chosen to co-mission with that has not blown it. Not one!

He truly is the redeemer of both us and our mission status. His motivation is to demonstrate the steadfastness of His perfect nature, the trustworthiness of His word to those who believe in Him, and as a testimony of these things to the onlookers around us who are yet believers.

Get in the Game

Sometime in the 1980s there was a movie released, titled *Short Circuit*. It was the story of a robot that became self-aware, not exactly an original plot. It was a feel-good movie though, and I've seen it more than once. One of the memorable lines from the movie was from the robot, dubbed "Number 5." After declaring, "Number 5 is alive," the robot developed a voracious appetite to learn, repeated in its request, "Need input."

Up until now we have focused on the completeness of the groundwork that God has already undertaken toward the success of your life mission(s). I dare say it would be possible for God to have ensured complete success without our input and involvement, but the truth is He has chosen for us to participate.

God has not chosen a robot, not even a self-aware robot, to carry out His purposes. He has chosen you and me. He has chosen people with flaws, doubts, fears, and even screwy ideas. He has chosen people who can say "No." Yet He has chosen wisely, because we can also choose to say "Yes," and mean it. God is not just about the end game, He is about the journey. His heart is, and has always been, about being in growing relationships with His maturing children. And the vehicle He chooses to achieve both those goals is by going on our mission with us. He has laid out His fantastical and perfect plan and says to us, "Need input."

It sounds absurd. That all-knowing God would require our input into the planning and execution of His plans toward His purposes doesn't make sense unless it is to take the opportunity to involve us in a family adventure with eternal meaning.

Do you feel inadequate? I do sometimes, but God has this to say to us through a psalm of David in Psalm 139:14:

> *"I will praise you for I am fearfully and wonderfully made; marvellous are your works, and that my soul knows very well."*

David appreciated the mastery of God's work within himself! Having a right understanding of this he then chose not to place himself on a shelf and admire God's handiwork. He repeatedly chose to work together with God to live out a life of significance, deliberately glorifying Him through purposeful living. He clearly didn't get it all right, but God was pleased (1Samuel 13:14, Acts 13:22).

David at times waited for God to reveal His plan and at times initiated his own plans and actions. David lived his life as a combination of God's presence and his own initiative.

We are called to do likewise. In Luke 14:25-33, the words of Christ to the crowd following Him are recalled. Christ's words are to highlight the absolute commitment required to follow Him. His two illustrations are of building and battling, which also indicate the need for us to plan ahead. As a part of planning we must consider the requirements involved and the resources we have to meet those requirements. With God, we are not expected to meet all of the requirements ourselves, but it is prudent to consider. By doing so we can faithfully utilize the resources in our lives and identify areas of lack where we must gather resources and trust God for His provision.

Our journey is a continual balancing act of faithfully handling the tangibles at hand and trusting God for what is beyond.

Get Out of the Way

So far, I have encouraged us to trust in God and His finely tuned, infallible planning for us. To add to that I've suggested that, since our lives are a "co-mission" with God, we should have input to the planning of our mission profile. We are not robots or slaves, but children called into the family enterprise by a benevolent Father.

Now let me add another twist into the mix.

You may have watched the movie, *Hidden Figures*. If not, allow me to recommend it. The story is based on a true story of a group of African-American, female mathematicians who worked at NASA in the organization's infancy. Their work was critical to the progress of NASA's program.

In one scene, there is a group discussion about what is known and what is not known about the calculations to put a manned craft into orbit and get it back down again safely.

One of the lead characters points out that they could get all the math right and then on the day, there could be a wind shift that changes everything.

Here is the twist.

God has made His plans. There is an expectation that we will contribute to that plan. God's desire is for us to have input into those plans and take an active responsibility in fulfilling them.

It seems to be, however, that when we invest in doing something, we shift toward making and trusting in processes, rather than in God and His likeness in us. When we identify an idea that works we tend to camp around it and enshrine it. The mathematicians in *Hidden Figures* eventually worked out the math to achieve their mission. They then had to learn to do the math on the fly to cope with variables like wind speed and direction on launch day.

We have to learn to do likewise. We need to learn to do the math too, and then adapt according to the conditions of our day. The Holy Spirit is sometimes described as wind. He blows where He will. It is essential that we be prepared to change our plans and calculations of how things are going to work out. It is imperative that we learn to move with what God is doing because He will shift the direction and speed of His activity and presence. He does so to keep us on target, considering conditions that only He can see from His unique perspective. Also, He is always working in us to establish trust and obedience.

As we discover and embrace God's plan for us, we become actively responsible within that plan, and we also stay flexible to change. You can see how necessary it is that at every step of our mission journey we are in close relationship with Him, to hear His voice for instruction and course corrections.

The Mission Community

While we each have to travel along our own trajectory, it should be clear by now that, along with God's planning and continual presence along the way, there is the need for a team greater than oneself to stay on course and complete our mission.

Before, during, and after a mission, astronauts are constantly interacting with the essential community around them that facilitates success. We need to be embedded in community where others are doing the behind the scenes work for our mission, such as training, advice, monitoring, situational awareness, time sensitive actions, and warnings. At the same time, we also are the necessary support crew for others' missions.

Collectively we share in each other's journeys. And we need one another. The Bible teaches us about one body with many parts working together for health and growth (Ephesians 4:11-16, 1 Corinthians 12:12-27, Romans 12:4-5).

We need community with others. In a community we have opportunities and challenges essential to our forward progress and the progress of others. We are not meant to live in a disconnect from relationships. These earthly relationships are a reflection of the harmonious relationship that exists between God the Father, Jesus, and the Holy Spirit. In our earthly relationships, we have the opportunity to prepare for the heavenly relationship that we are invited into.

Therefore we have the privilege of playing instructor and inspirer, educator and encourager, friend, advocate, confidant, counsellor, and more to each other for the benefit of God's bigger, BIGGER purposes.

One thing becomes quite clear in studying how space programs play out. It is not about the astronaut.

Astronauts are often the public face of a mission. They can be the most conspicuous person in their mission community, sometimes playing the role of public relations officer along with their main job description. Because of this they can appear to be more important than their mission colleagues. The truth is that greater visibility doesn't necessarily mean greater importance. It would be easy to elevate them above the crowd. It would be easy for an astronaut to esteem themselves above others considering their higher profile roles…But that would be a mistake.

From reading the personal accounts from astronauts there seems to be an almost universal understanding that they are one person among many, working toward a purpose far greater than their individual selves. There is even an appreciation for the rare opportunities they have in the context of a much bigger picture with a lot more people.

Astronauts know that it is not about the astronaut.

We need to remember that our life journey is also about something bigger than ourselves and it includes a community with whom we co-mission.

While God shapes us and loves us throughout, the journey is not just about us.

My trajectory is not about me!

Logistics and mission requirements are formulated in the laboratory, alongside the training that every astronaut must successfully undergo to be mission ready. So, our next phase is training.

Planning the *Trajectory* Book

Once I had decided to write *Trajectory*, I needed to have a plan to make it happen. Fortunately, I had some free time for about 40 days after committing to write. That time opportunity helped set a goal to finish, which I didn't even come close to hitting, but it did get me started and kept me moving to the point of being invested in the result enough to not quit.

The format has evolved somewhat in the writing, but the original plan included chapters drawn directly from that "Trajectory" imagine in my mind. You know—the picture that I decided to paint, before realizing I didn't know how to paint.

Of course, writing a book is only a part of the picture. Editing and formatting have to take place for the work to be presentable. Choices need to be made about how and where to publish. Finally, are the promotional considerations for the completed work. These plans can continue well beyond the actual writing phase of the book.

It's easy to see how planning out even the simplest vision can become a much larger scenario than the original vision detail. This is a part of the process of bringing a vision into reality, and can be quite intimidating—even discouraging—as you think of new areas that need to be addressed.

The planning phase is where all the detail for your vision is laid out on the table and organized into a workable sequence from your starting point through to your mission destination. Ideally, as this process is worked through, all the gaps and deficiencies in the plan are highlighted and addressed prior to execution.

Planning Checklist

1. Can you describe what you think are the main features of God's trajectory for you?

2. Do you trust in His plan for you?

3. Consider the main people and events that have positively or negatively shaped your ability to trust. Ask

God to help in this process. Talk to Him about how to imitate the positive examples. Ask for His help to separate our ability to trust Him, from those events and people who might have made it difficult to trust.

4. What are the personal responsibilities you have in walking out His plan for you? (Be as detailed as possible, bearing in mind that you can only see part of your forward journey.)

5. What is the next step in your unique journey?

6. Psalm 139 reveals the psalmist's awareness of himself being a part of God's marvellous works. How do you see yourself?

7. Are you willing to take the next step?

8. What can you prepare today, for tomorrow?

9. Can you think of a time you have enshrined a part of your plan and process?

10. How can you stay flexible to change?

11. Who do you have in your planning and support crew community?

12. Whose mission are you supporting?

13. Have you ever felt like the mission needs to be completely aborted because you've gone so hopelessly off course or failed in spectacular fashion?

14. If yes to the previous question, what steps did you take, or can you take to restart your mission and get back on course?

15. Can you take a vision for your future and begin to proceed through planning?

16. What is God saying to you through the planning chapter?

17. Ask for His help through your planning process. Ask Him to provide for and give guidance for your journey.

Training—Personal Preparation

I made an amazing discovery while researching this book!

The Kennedy Space Centre in Florida has a program called "Astronaut Training Experience" or "ATX" (astronauts love acronyms). It's a program that allows non-astronaut types, like me, to play at being an astronaut for a few hours.

Astronaut Training Experience! Do I hear "bucket list," anyone? I'm thinking of starting a donation website to help get me there. Any takers?

There is actually a good lesson for us here. Pretty much anyone aged eight and older can attend ATX and go through certain simulated activities that mimic actual astronaut training. No matter how many times an individual participates in ATX, though, they would not be ready to become an astronaut.

Sometimes we can get caught up in going through the motions and fill our lives with seemingly worthwhile activities, thinking we are in mission training, only to discover that we've just been a tourist at a simulated experience that makes no real contribution to our forward progress at all.

Whether it be making a new discovery about your future (*Stargazing*), working out the way to get there (*The Laboratory*), or being accepted into Astronaut *Training*, these new discoveries and beginnings normally come with a healthy dose of fear and doubt, which in the first place is normally overridden by the euphoria of the exciting and new!

The space training centre element of taking flight and following a very specific and individual trajectory toward a predetermined mission, is potentially the most difficult of all of the aspects of our purposeful journeys through life. As such it is also the place where euphoria can quickly turn to despair, determination to a loss of will to continue, and from thinking (with puffed chest), "I'm an astronaut," to "I'm a loser."

While stargazing at our potential future, failure seldom enters the equation. Failures identified in the laboratory are seen as part of the process of eliminating superfluous items and activity from the mission. Failures in the laboratory stage are wins because they prevent mistakes being made.

Space training centre however, is where things get more personal. Failures here can be received as failures and flaws in our very identity.

Individuals who make it into NASA astronaut training are referred to as AsCans, short for Astronaut Candidates, and are immensely qualified. Not just anybody gets accepted. The standards and requirements are exceptionally high. Those who meet the initial application requirements are then put through weeks of gruelling interviews, screenings, and orientations, before qualifying as AsCans and commencing the real training.

The standards and requirements to follow your predetermined flight path to your life purpose are higher. But in Christ you are pre-qualified, read 2 Corinthians 5:21:

> *"For He made Him who knew no sin to be sin for us, that we might become the righteousness of God in Him."*

God is calling you righteous -don't argue. You are righteous, and that righteousness does not depend on you feeling righteous. Jesus exchanged our ugly, death-inducing sin for His own righteousness. His righteousness restores our relationship with the original star maker and stargazer. We are thus qualified to undergo training toward the predetermined course to the works that God, the master planner, has already mapped out in every detail. And so, we qualify for God's Space Training Academy.

If we are prequalified in Christ, then why is it that failure seems to be such a constant companion throughout the process, and why do we need such training?

Highly qualified non-astronauts attend their respective space programs to become highly qualified astronauts. Just as a highly qualified non-astronaut has no way of successfully being an astronaut without rigorous training, a highly qualified you and me have no way of traversing through life to successful mission completion without the right training.

Failures in training do not mean we no longer qualify. They highlight that we need more training.

Remember Romans 11:29:

"For the gifts and the calling of God are irrevocable."

We may quit or fail to complete our mission, but God never takes it away from us.

The need for more training is possibly the greatest reason why failures and setbacks take place. When I was an apprentice mechanic, I was, in terms of being a mechanic, as dumb as a post. Each new encounter seemed to highlight my lack of knowledge and experience. Fortunately, my employers had realistic expectations (most of the time), and patiently worked with me over four years to make me a competent mechanic. There were many times though, that I felt inadequate and feared that I would never become a mechanic.

It helps us to keep progressing by bearing in mind this truth. The very purpose of training is to show our flaws and inadequacies so they can be equipped and eliminated, or at least managed.

Training is a pathway to transformation.

I remember sitting on the tractor with my uncle who was plowing over some previously unfarmed ground, again and again. I asked him why he kept going around and round over the same dirt. He replied that he kept going over the same ground until no more rocks and tree roots came to the surface. Then he would know that the field was ready for planting.

Please allow me a friendly warning here. The plow was not dragging up the past. It was bringing to the surface potential obstacles that lay hidden and could impede the success of the crop.

In our own lives, allow the Holy Spirit to be the plow. He knows what lurks within us and knows the where, what, and when of our hidden obstacles. Without His direction, we can spend our lives in fruitless, internal searches that leave us being just another sweaty, frustrated person standing in the middle of our field with a shovel and no clue.

We can often approach training with a mindset to tick all the right boxes, or at least enough to pass, while avoiding any embarrassing failures. In reality, we should embrace our failures as part of the learning and refining process that they are.

And remember, accepting your failures and acknowledging your limitations along with your need to be taught, displays true humility and grace. James 4:6:

"God resists the proud, but gives grace to the humble."

Be realistic about where you are in your training and God will help you. That's a sweet deal!

A Final Word on Failure

Romans 8:28:

> *"And we know that all things work together for good, to those who love God, to those who are the called, according to His purpose."*

All things, even failure, setbacks and course corrections, work together for good.

Basic Training

The amount of time that AsCans spend in training depends to some degree on the specific missions they are chosen for, but all of them commence with a two-year initial training period. Beyond this, training is tailored to suit the specific mission and the specific role that each AsCan will play in those missions. For example, astronauts training for long duration missions aboard the International Space Station (ISS), undergo additional training of between two to three years on top of basic training. (Long duration missions on ISS are considered to be 3-6 months long.) In short, their training is ongoing.

For us too, our training may have some defined periods with a specific beginning and end, but it will also be made up of a lifetime of ongoing training and learning events.

All of the AsCans go through the basic two years of training that follows the selection process. It's not the timeframe that is important when we contemplate our own personal training, but the "basic" or foundational elements that additional training is built upon.

Luke 6:46-48 gives us a picture of the contents of that foundational training:

> *"But why do you call me "Lord, Lord," and do not do the things I say? Whoever comes to me, and here's my sayings and does them, I will show you whom he is like: He is like a man building a house, who dug deep and laid the foundation on the rock. And when the flood arose, the stream beat vehemently against that house, and could not shake it, for it was founded on the rock."*

Personal Trajectory Training 101

"Lord, Lord," - Jesus starts this conversation with His followers with the premise that they call Him Lord. In fact, His question implies it is possible for them, for us, to call Him Lord, but not actually treat Him as Lord.

This is the first of the foundational truths that we must realize and understand. While we have a will and must manage ourselves with the self-control available to us (Galatians 5:22), we must know that He is our mission commander. I'd love to tell you that I am the perfect example of correctly recognizing His authority, but that would be a massive overstatement.

"and do not do the things I say?" - Obedience to Him is the direct measure He uses as evidence of our surrender to Him. Here we have a yardstick to help us measure our progress through basic training.

"hears" - Jesus points out firstly that we are in proximity to Him to be able to hear Him. Relationship with Christ is everything! (John 15) Secondly, that we can and should have the expectation that He will speak to us, and thirdly that we are actually paying attention. Coming back to relationship, we will hear and understand because we are close enough to Him relationally to understand His heart in what He says.

"does them"—If we didn't hear it the first time, obedient action is one of the outcomes of our training.

Jesus then continues His discussion with a further illustration for what the training looks like and the end results.

"like a man building a house"- we too are building; not a house, but a life of purpose. While most of the focus can be on the construction phase of building a house, there is much that comes before and after.

"who dug deep and laid the foundation on the rock" -If nothing else, we should realize that "basic" training doesn't mean "easy." Digging is one of my least favorite jobs! Digging out the old to get in touch with the bedrock of a life built on Christ is no easy feat either. In essence, what we are doing here is removing the things in our life that we have previously trusted in or built upon. They may include false belief systems, reliance on material things like money or possessions, status, occupation, etc., and replacing them with the foundations of God's kingdom. Here our first layer of foundation is us at the cross; realizing our need for salvation, before a loving God who has reached out to us through His own sacrifice.

Jesus then describes the finished building being able to withstand whatever life throws at it. A house standing in the face of adversity, in this case, represents a life of enduring strength.

Basic training is about establishing our connection with and reliance on God and the resultant strength and quality of character; the foundation and the house.

While our basic training all has the same end goal, the process looks different for each of us and the timeframe varies, too. We are all different and so require different methods of teaching for God to instil the basics into us.

In addition to this, God has His eye on lining up key timelines for our mission. We may feel like we are proceeding or growing slowly, but God is lining us up with His perfect timing always. (Acts 17:26, Romans 5:6)

Building upon the foundations of basic training, AsCans also receive what might best be described as contextual training. They must learn every relevant piece of information about their responsibilities and the systems around them while on mission.

Training begins with reading training manuals and taking tests. This sounds pretty boring, comparatively. It would be easy for an astronaut to protest, "Hey, I came here to bravely go where no man has gone before, not have my head stuck in an earth-bound book for years!"

It's easy for us to protest that our grand plans of world changing service to God seem to be bogged down in an apparently mundane existence. We need to read the training manual. The Bible is our training manual and we can never afford to become less acquainted with it. Always, we must become more acquainted with it. Through it, we become more closely aligned with our mission commander and develop the trust required to stay on mission. We learn what it is to be a co-worker with God. We learn our true identity and we also learn our personal mission specifics.

Following is a sample list of training requirements with a parallel for those of us in training for our Godly mission.

Learn Russian

I don't know where this fits into the curriculum, but it is an obvious inclusion, considering that all flights to the ISS are currently aboard Soviet craft.

What does this highlight for us? We need to learn to communicate. Almost universally, we are poor communicators, and the more important the conversation is, the worse we typically become.

A couple of years ago, as a part of my research to help marriages, I conducted a survey of women regarding men. The standout response that eclipsed all others to questions regarding what women wanted men to do better was you guessed it, "communicate."

The bad news is that sometimes when we speak the same language as someone (E.g. English), we can assume that everything we say is heard as we intend it, and every word we hear, we understand as the speaker intended. A number of variables mean this is not always so.

The good news is we can learn communication skills (speaking and listening) and practice them in the same way we would learn and practice a new language, like Russian.

Part of our difficulty with communication is that we think everyone else thinks like us and wants the same things. Big mistake!

While I spent many years criticizing the practice of personality profiling, I can now see some value in the practice. My criticism, which can still be valid, was that it puts people into boxes that some might never escape from. I suspect now my real reason was that I didn't really know who I was, and I wasn't entirely sure that I'd like the answer presented to me. So, I thought it was best to be like a mushroom and stay in the dark about such matters.

Anyhow, I think perhaps the greater value, or at least of equal value, in personality type discoveries, is in understanding others so we can better communicate with them. We can avoid situations where we think we are being helpful but aren't.

ISS (International Space Station) and Spacecraft Systems Training

The training focuses on astronauts being able to use and monitor on-board systems, recognize when a fault exists, and take remedial action.

In our case, we have powerful on-board systems too. Our ability to think is unrivalled in all of earthly creation. Remember whose image we have been made in. Add to this our unique will, character, and our powerful spirit, and we are as God says, "fearfully and wonderfully made."

God has provided us with our internal monitoring system of conscience. (Romans 2:12-15)

Ground stations externally monitor ISS systems as well, to provide another set of eyes to watch the system's health and mission progress. God has gifted us with each other, His Body, to provide meaningful and timely feedback to aid in correctly interpreting input. The importance for us to remain in connection with each other is paramount.

And as if that is not enough, God has sealed the deal by sending us the Holy Spirit. (2 Corinthians 1:20-22)

If we correctly use the systems God has designed into us, maintain mature and healthy relationships with our fellow believers, program our faculties with life giving data from the training manual, and heed the voice of the Holy Spirit, mission success is guaranteed!

Notice that a primary course objective for Astronauts in training is to be able to take the correct action in the right timeframe. In space, there is no breakdown service. If you can't act appropriately when necessary, you are more likely to experience "game over" than mission success.

We are equipped and fully supported for mission success, but we must take responsibility and act.

Extravehicular Activity Skills Training

Astronauts generally undertake extravehicular activities to fulfil mission requirements or make repairs, so these skills are essential. As with the previous training element, the emphasis here is taking action.

This training component reminds me of the time Jesus came walking on the water to the disciples in the boat. Peter asked to join Jesus on the water, with mixed results. The first key here is, like the space-walking astronaut, we must sometimes leave the relative safety and comfort of our craft, our current position, to pursue something greater. Secondly, when we step out, when we act, it must be action borne of faith, not action borne of fear. As Peter's example shows, there are two very different results. (Matthew 14:25-33)

Aircraft Flight Readiness Training

In my earlier years, I used to avoid checklists like the plague! I remember having to perform vehicle services using them and because I didn't see the value in them, I would often cut corners. Usually I got away with it.

Flight readiness training ensures that the craft is actually ready for flight and that any essential input from the crew for successful lift-off is completed. There is no room here for shortcuts, oversights or mistakes.

In my latter years, I've come to appreciate how checklists and procedures help me to do a complete job in a methodical manner. In fact, nowadays I get to contribute to formulating procedures.

Your personal mission that is reached along your individualized trajectory is also put at risk by not operating in God's orderly manner. The risk to your success is too great to warrant taking shortcuts.

Antigravity and G-force Training

Astronauts are subjected to the kind of conditions they will experience in space, and the journey there and back. Before an astronaut straps in for their mission, they must be tested to find that their individual body can both handle the pressure of launch and be able to function in weightlessness.

Let's call ourselves, "Theo-nauts" (God-voyagers). Do you like that? I just made it up.

For us Theo-nauts, we too must learn to deal with the immense pressure that we are sometimes subjected to. NASA has devised purpose-built machines and aerial manoeuvres in modified aircraft to achieve its training objectives. God, at times, is far less subtle. Life and circumstance are His tools to test us under immense pressure and to see how we cope in the antigravity of isolation, like the weightless astronaut, without any visible means of support.

Choosing this perspective during trying times can help us go on, knowing that the trial will indeed end and it will bear fruit in us. At the same time, tests and trials reveal to our encouraging Father and ourselves that, yes, indeed we are maturing in His kingdom. This is good and necessary news! (Romans 5:1-5)

In fact, we can endure and also take courage that our Father has His eye on us. He is close by, willing our success even as an earthly father wills his children on as they take their first steps, remove the training wheels, graduate, marry, etc. The Father's joy never ends.

Survival Training and Life Support Systems

Astronaut training includes knowing the on-board systems that sustain their lives while on mission, and the practical steps to take when encountering possible unplanned scenarios.

For example, among so many other things, astronauts have to have a minimum swimming skill level. Hold on—I'm not sure if NASA realizes there are no beaches in space, and definitely no spa on the ISS!

Yes, they do realize; but they also realize that a craft can end up over water on re-entry and astronauts may have to evacuate the capsule to survive.

Theo-nauts also have to prepare for eventualities that are, from their perspective at least, unplanned.

God, of course, knows exactly how it will pan out and He probably chooses not to share all of the detail with us upfront, to save the tops of our heads exploding with too much information.

Therefore an astronaut must have a skill—swimming—that seems totally unnecessary for his or her mission.

The same is true for us. Learning and growing opportunities arrive that we can turn our nose up to because it is outside our projected mission parameters and requirements. Let's look at some possible scenarios.

A business friend is struggling with promotional materials, and you are a marketing guru. You could see opportunity to serve, or think, "But no, marketing is just my day job, I'm really called to heal the sick".

There is a need for extra helpers in children's ministry at your local church. You could either think that would be an unnecessary disruption to your talents that you are honing to become an artist for the Lord, or give it a try and have everything you thought you knew about creativity blown out of the water by the liberated expression of these young humans.

You're driving to meet a Godly woman for a date that you believe is "The One." You pass a car pulled over the side of the road with a flat tire and the driver clearly could use some assistance. You have the time and the ability. Do you stop?

Every opportunity that you encounter to be involved in a situation isn't necessarily for you, and every request for help does not have to be met with a "yes," no matter who the request comes from.

How then do you decide? A common-sense approach is a good place to start. Do you have, or could you learn the skills/requirements? What would be the downside of taking the opportunity? How does it fit with your current responsibilities?

The relationship with God remains paramount, always.

Survival training is important, because dead astronauts don't complete missions.

Life in Space Skills

Spacecraft are confined spaces forcing people to live in close proximity in an unnatural environment. Everyday tasks in space take on a whole new perspective. Astronauts need to know how to cope in this environment and perform such mundane tasks as eat, take care of personal hygiene, and exercise, all while in micro-gravity.

We too must learn to function normally in situations that are not normal. Astronauts sojourn in an unnatural environment. We travel in a supernatural environment which can be just as disorienting.

Practice and persistence are the keys.

You can see how this extensive training naturally leads into the mission specific training that will take place as AsCans graduate to become astronauts.

Likewise, our individual training looks less and less generic as we proceed toward our specific mission.

Consider the characters throughout history as recorded in the Bible. Some share similarities in their preparation and the lives they lived, while other lives are worlds apart. The vast array of examples is there to teach us, and in part to remind us that there is no one-size-fits-all. There is no universal formula that works the same way for everyone, every time.

What there is, is this marvellous mystery of the sovereignty of God working together with the freewill He has given us. It is a perfectly peculiar combination that can guarantee mission success.

Rebels With a Cause

Have you ever seen the movie, *The Right Stuff*? It's a movie that follows the early years of the US space program, and the focus of the storyline is on the selection and training of potential astronauts. The initial pool of astronaut candidates was drawn primarily from elite military pilots, because these men were deemed to have "The Right Stuff." These men were characterized by their formidable flight skills, physical fitness, and courage, but there was also something else.

They had a willingness to break the rules. When told that the sound barrier couldn't be broken they went out and flew through it. Many sacrificed their lives in that pursuit. When told that a demon lived out there at the speed of Mach 1, they went out to meet it and overcome it.

In the story, there was some resistance to selecting fighter pilots as astronaut candidates because they were considered difficult to deal with. These men didn't always toe the line or follow orders

What these men displayed was a willingness to break the rules. Sometimes they broke them because they were too full of themselves. Other times they broke them because they knew what was required in the moment to survive or progress. I believe the space race would not have fared as well had it not been for the imperfect men who were willing to say, "I know the rule book says this, but this is the way I am going to do it."

These men were characterized by "The Right Stuff," which included rebelliousness toward the things that would have kept them from their destiny.

In my early years, I was so scared of getting into trouble. I'm not sure where that fear came from, but while others would have seen me as a "good boy," I was just too scared to deliberately do anything wrong. This fear of doing wrong extended to the way I related to people. Seen as a nice person and a bit of a peacemaker, I was really just scared of being offside with people and being rejected.

For the best part of my early life I strived to be a "nice person," not because I actually was a nice person, just a scared person, not wanting to be found in the wrong. Another observation from my early life is that I also didn't achieve much and lived with a frustration that I wasn't living up to the undefined potential that I felt was locked up inside me. I believe there is a direct relationship between my early fearful compliance and my early lack of productivity.

To be honest, when I first became a Christian, these attributes went into overdrive. I thought a Christian should surely be super nice and super compliant and obedient. But then a funny thing began to happen. As my relationship with Christ deepened and my understanding of His words expanded, I began to lean into His heart behind the laws that govern us. I began to understand the purpose of rules and laws. They are there to serve us. Rules are there to preserve life and relationship, not to be a measure of our spirituality or worth. Romans chapter 3 is a good place to consider what God is saying to you about how you relate to laws.

In more recent years I have been less concerned with rules and people's opinions of me, and more concerned with finding the right way forward. In recent years, I am also much more productive and content with my progress.

In 1Samuel 21:1-6, David asks for bread from the priest. The only bread that was available was the bread of the presence which David and his men were forbidden to eat. In verse five David voices his adherence to one law and in verse 6 he breaks another by accepting the holy bread. David loved God, understood His heart and knew what was important. Clearly, David didn't always get it right, but he knew in his heart what was right or wrong.

Am I saying that the end always justifies the means? No. Am I saying that obedience and discipline is not important? No. Am I suggesting we should adopt "situational ethics" and just do what feels right in the moment? No. Am I saying that rules and laws don't matter? No.

What I am saying is that as we get to know Him more we begin to act out of His law written in our hearts rather than something external. As we grow in this we will be rightful responders to God more than robotic adherers to rules. I am saying that rules and laws are servants to preserve life and relationship and I am saying that we must know when God's heart overrides law in a given set of circumstances.

Just as each of our paths is unique, so too is each of our relationships with rules and law in our personal journey. Cultivating our relationship with God and learning to recognize His voice is our safeguard.

I was hesitant to write this section, knowing the potential for some to receive my words as license to do as they please. In pushing ahead, I have weighed up that danger against the absolute necessity for us to proceed along our trajectories by faithfully navigating rules and laws.

Training for Writing the *Trajectory* Book

At the age of eight my grasp on the English language was, shall we say, limited. Some may agree that not much has changed and on occasions where I am doing a poor job of using my native language, I would be forced to agree!

One of the foundational areas of training for writing this book has been learning the language. Like most training, this is an ongoing process. Luckily, learning how to make paper age well has not been a required skill to complete this particular mission, because I completely failed at that.

There are many more skills required to complete the writing task that include computing skills, formatting for my chosen format of Kindle, promotional knowhow, and many more. One of the keys to success is knowing when you can outsource some of the skills required. For my first book, I had a cover design concept in mind. I presented the idea to a professional designer who humored me by mocking up a presentation of my concept alongside a couple of her own ideas that she had. Let's just say I was quick to realize why she was the professional.

Add to that the life and social skills required to function and relate well with integrity, and you have quite a mission on your hands. Abilities and qualities acquired then need to be trained, maintained, and developed further.

Taking a snapshot of my current ability to complete writing a book through to publishing, I know there is massive potential to improve, and that is ok.

Training Checklist

1. How do we tell the difference between actual training, and pointless and sometimes endless simulations? Can you find an example in your own life? (Hint: are

your activities bearing results in line with your mission progress?)

2. Can you identify some things in your life that could be considered failures? Ask God to reveal to you how He has positively shaped your training and trajectory by those things. Forgive yourself.

3. Do you find you have frequent misunderstandings when communicating?

4. If yes, it might be time to skill up your communication.

5. Remember the opportunity scenarios I ran past you? How would you answer them?

6. It's important for you to know why you answered #5 the way you did.

7. Are there opportunities or requests before you that may need a revisit?

8. Consider the development of your character. Can you identify some areas of character development thus far? Can you identify areas of your character that need work to not only complete your mission, but to travel well? What can you do to aid this growing process?

9. Consider some of the abilities required for successful completion of your mission(s). Make a list of abilities acquired and in development. Include even basic, foundational skills. Can you think of abilities that are still lacking?

10. How can you work on these areas?

11. Astronaut training is very focused on appropriate action. List all of the appropriate action(s) you can begin in this session.

12. Thinking about the training modules mentioned and how they relate to the "Theo-naut," can you relate experiences in your life to training in those areas?

13. When you are faced with difficulty, do you sometimes need to shift your perspective from, "Woe is me," to "God is in this, I will get through this and be better for the experience?" (I know I do!)

14. Taking a snapshot of yourself right now, can you acknowledge room for improvement but still be ok with who you are at this moment?

15. How would you describe your relationship to rules and laws? Does anything need to change?

16. What is God saying to you through the training chapter?

17. Ask God to help you identify training opportunities as they arrive.

18. Ask God for His help in your training.

Launch – Getting Started

Years pass by as the vision to reach for more is planned into existence and as the individual voyager has the mission trained into them.

Because astronaut training and preparation is so tactile, it probably rarely seems to them as if they are not working toward their mission.

For us though, the training can be so subtle and feel so slow, it is commonplace to have times of serious doubt that you will get to do anything but train. We can find ourselves wondering if we had only imagined that we were called to be prepared for a mission to God's Kingdom. If you've ever entertained these ideas, you are not alone, and you are completely normal.

But if we submit to the training process and do not give up, launch day eventually comes around.

Your Starting Point

Obviously, launch day is not the beginning of a space mission. Likewise, most of us are busy living our lives when the idea of greater purpose and personal mission arrive on our radar. By that stage we have usually formed many opinions about how things work and who we are. Some of these opinions are wrong or at least irrelevant.

The ongoing significance of our personal origins can be one area where we hold on to distorted realities of our identity and capacity for any worthwhile achievement.

Researching the backgrounds of many astronauts I discovered that they come from a myriad of backgrounds. They come from a multitude of variables including family circumstances, race, gender, birthplace and more. Basically, astronauts are made from people.

My point is that your starting point may dictate the direction you set off in, but it doesn't have to determine how far you go or your level of experience and influence along the way. Let us consider the story of Gideon.

Gideon's story begins in Judges 6:11. If you have a Bible handy, have a read through until at least verse 26. The conversation between Gideon and the angel is very revealing.

Gideon believes things about himself and God based in the facts of his life

It is as if the angel doesn't hear Gideon's assessment of things. The angel speaks to the true Gideon who is not defined by his circumstances and he speaks of a God who is close by.

The angel then calls Gideon into a mission with Godly purpose, and without judgement, meets Gideon where he is.

What a remarkable story of encouragement for those of us with inglorious pasts, and seemingly unlikely starting points for our destiny. Your starting point is not the determiner of your ultimate destiny.

Pre-launch

Launch day arrives, and from what I understand, there is a whole lot of waiting around while someone else decides when to light the candle underneath you.

The website howwelivestories.com interviewed American astronaut Mike Good, asking him what it was like to go into space. His responses highlight some of the prelaunch detail from a perspective that most of the rest of us can only imagine.

He describes his mood during the van ride out to the launch as sombre. That mood was not of fear but a sense of the importance of the job at hand, and an awareness that it is "a little risky." A little risky? This guy must have ice water running through his veins to make an understatement like that! He says he was focused but excited.

His response when asked if he was scared was, *"I wasn't really scared, I was just very focused and excited, anticipating this big event."*

What a great way to view his situation, to view any situation. What a great way to view our current phase of our unique trajectories.

God tells us many times in His word, not to fear. He doesn't say that there won't be situations that could induce fear.

Jesus would likely have slept through the storm on the lake described in Mathew 8:24-27, had it not been for being awakened by his frightened travelling companions. His response was to scold them for their lack of faith. Could a fierce storm on a lake be dangerous? Yes, but like Mike Good, who considered the launch into his journey "a little risky," Jesus had the right perspective. A potentially dangerous storm up against the power and authority of the Son of God? I can imagine Jesus yawning at the prospect.

Jesus is with us in the journey, just as He was in the boat with the disciples. And He will remain with us through all the situations that we will encounter that are likely to incite fear in us (Isaiah 43:1-2).

Mike Good and astronauts like him put their potential fear up against the creative power of the original mission vision;

the exhaustive planning and preparation that has brought him to launch and the greater purpose he understands is behind his current experience. These things, coupled with the dedicated and highly competent community of people who are co-workers in the mission, diminish the risks and any fear he may experience down to merely, "a little risky."

All of these aspects are applicable for us too. But the greatest leveller of our fears is the who behind us, alongside us, and inside us. The who in whose image we have been made, and who has called us onto mission with Him.

Not fearful; but focused should be the result of our big picture awareness of what is at stake, what our role is, and what resources are at our disposal.

Jesus risked all for us. We cannot expect to serve out our particular trajectory through space and time without being exposed to risk. I mean actual risk; the risk of losing something, someone, or even one's own life. Remember the response of the ruler to his servant who, through fear, avoided taking a risk with his talent and buried it (Matthew 25:14-30). Remember also, Mordecai's words to Esther (Esther 4:13-14). Without risk, there is no reward.

Here are some more comments from Mike Good.

"The space shuttle launch is a really exciting time for us. It's like our Super Bowl. We've trained really hard for this, and it's a big deal for us. We want to do well. We want to win the game."

Taking the next step, the next really big, really fast step in our journey toward completing our life mission(s) comes, as with the astronauts, feelings of excitement and a sense of the gravity (no pun intended) of the occasion. These perspectives are held with a desire to execute well.

Author Daniel Pink says that two of the three primary motivators for humans are the desire to excel and to work toward a cause greater than oneself. If Mike Good's description holds true for his colleagues, it seems that astronauts epitomize these motivators.

If Daniel Pink is right, and I suspect he is, it would seem that we are wired to want to live a life of significance, a life that is bigger than ourselves. It makes sense that God made us that way, so that we would not just be willing, but we would seek out opportunity to go further and do more with Him. We are designed with drivers inside us that would push us from the lead weight of inertia, through the trials of training, and on to executing our missions of eternal significance.

As an astronaut, you dress up for the launch and then you wait for the van to take you to the launch site. There, you wait your turn to be strapped into the craft. You then wait for the launch crew to perform some final checks and then seal the door. Hours roll past as the prelaunch process continues, and the astronauts, after already investing so much effort over many years, have to wait some more.

Waiting really is sometimes the name of the game, for astronauts and theo-nauts alike. Waiting is one thing, but waiting patiently is what is really required—by launch control and by God. There can be a multitude of reasons for delays to take place, but we can rest assured that God is using holdups, setbacks, and postponements to continue the internal work of our hearts. God is mindful of our mission, but He will not sacrifice the state of our heart for mission. The state of our heart and our relationship with Him are core to His big picture purpose.

Oh, the joys of waiting for something that you are really excited for—said no one, ever!

Oh, and did I mention the physical discomfort while you're waiting? Mike Good does.

> *"The orange pressure suits that we wear for launch and re-entry have air bottles in them, and you're lying on your parachute and it's kind of lumpy. You're sitting shoulder to shoulder with your fellow crewmembers, and it's also kind of a weird position to be in."*

Sounds divine!

All of the awkwardness that you may experience in your launch position may be highly uncomfortable, but the purpose of those inclusions was never meant for your comfort. They are meant for your survival. Spacesuit designers aren't evil people wishing to inflict pain on their clients. They do what is required to get their clients through their mission without dying. Equally, God is not evil and has as His primary focus your survival through to mission completion. He desires to see your trajectory go full course.

One last pre-launch word from Mike Good:

"On my last mission, I was the last one to get strapped in, so I had time to hang out at the pad at the 195-foot level while I was waiting to get in the vehicle. It's a beautiful view up there. I took in the breeze, looked out at the Florida coastline, and thought about how in a couple of hours, this rocket was going to launch me off the planet. It was pretty cool."

I love the fact that at this time of intense focus, Mike was able to recognize the moment within the moment. Being able to appreciate windows of opportunity to stop and smell the roses makes the mission experience that much richer, and when shared, makes another's mission story that much more relatable.

It can be very easy to become so focused on the mission at hand and the particular demands in this moment, and the next, and the next...ad infinitum. You may have met people who are so serious about what they are doing that they are difficult to be around and almost impossible to relate to. Others may be so passionate about their mission that spending time in their company is like spending time in a closed room that is slowly having the atmosphere sucked out of it. Maybe you have a tendency to do likewise?

Focus is essential for achievement, that's a given, but it must find its balance. Not allowing oneself to change gears, or even coast when circumstance allows it, can leave the Theonaut with a bent that can see them become unnecessarily isolated, dull, and one dimensional.

Not everyone will understand your unique mission, let alone be interested in it, so be sure to limit the way and the amount you do share. Doing this also creates space in conversation and relationships to show value to, and even encourage others, with their mission story.

You are more than your mission.

Remember that God has called us into relationship with Him in His Kingdom family. We have not merely been conscripted into the family enterprise to take our place as just another cog in a heavenly machine.

The Launch

From reading firsthand accounts of manned rocket launches and viewing footage of the same, my view is that they are the epitome of deliberate and directional power.

A launch is a bit like a piece of orchestral music reaching the crescendo. All individuals and components working together in perfectly timed unison to deliver that musical power.

I watched as rocket engine nozzles shifted around as engines started and the power came on. In fact, this movement is controlled movement of the nozzle heads to provide steering for the craft. The steering is designed and directed to safely get the craft off the ground and to its next critical point.

Likewise, our missions are launched with an incredible power that is beyond our own. The forcefulness comes from a power outside us and is beyond our sole capacity to direct in a meaningful way. Thinking of it in these terms makes the idea of trusting God a far more logical conclusion than trying to maintain outright control ourselves.

I'm not suggesting we relinquish all control of our lives. Rather, to relax into God's guidance over a power only He can provide, directing us on our respective missions along the right trajectory. Astronauts have responsibility and input into the progress through the phases of their specific mission, but it is in the context of the overall mission objective as agreed with mission control and in harmony with all of the inputs and responsibilities of all of the rest of the community who are a part of the same mission.

At times, and launch is one of those times, astronauts are more passenger than participant in their destiny. Right at the point and execution of launch, they are really only controlling themselves in the midst of all the activity that is going on around them. Our life journey is very similar in that there are times when control is all but removed from our hands and all that is required of us is to manage ourselves within what could be seen as a chaotic environment.

The idea of an astronaut taking control over their craft mid-launch is inconceivable, but how many times have we interrupted our own launch process by, for want of a better word, interfering.

The website, Businessinsider.com.au ran a story where Canadian astronaut Chris Hadfield describes what a shuttle launch is like. I imagine the experience would be similar in any of the craft that have been able to escape gravity to Earth's orbit. You may remember astronaut Chris for his video at the ISS singing David Bowie's "Space Oddity." Cool guy, cool song—check it out on YouTube.

Here is an excerpt from that article:

> *"Launch is immensely powerful, and you can truly feel yourself in the centre of it, like riding an enormous wave, or being pushed and lifted by a huge hand, or shaken in the jaws of a gigantic dog. The vehicle shakes and vibrates, and you are pinned hard down into your seat by the acceleration. As one set of engines [stops] and the next starts, you are thrown forward and then shoved back. The weight of over 4gs for many minutes is oppressive, like an enormous fat person lying on you, until suddenly, after 9 minutes, the engine shut off and you are instantly weightless. Magic. Like a gorilla was squishing you and then threw you off a cliff. Quite a ride."*

What a great description from someone who has experienced it!

That is what you feel when you are breaking the bounds of Earth's gravitational pull by accelerating from zero to 17,500 miles an hour (28,160kilometres per hour) in 8.5 to 9 minutes.

I've driven some fast cars, but that redefines fast. It sounds as violent as it does powerful and as exhilarating as it does overwhelming.

Acceleration, massive acceleration, is the main feature of the launch.

After long years of work and, it would seem, many hours waiting around on launch day, the astronauts are finally flung into orbit.

Mike Good describes it this way:

> *"When you get to nine minutes from launch, things start happening really fast. Time speeds up — it feels like just a few seconds. The engines light and you just get kicked off that pad."*

It's funny how time seems to be elastic, depending on what is happening. I'm sure we can all relate to times where if feels like the clock has stopped and other times we are left wondering where it went.

Our personal trajectory, like the astronauts, is not lived out at one steady pace. It would be a mistake to think so. Times, even extended seasons, can be spent wondering if any real progress is even happening, and then suddenly, we get kicked off the pad, like Mike Good and his fellow travellers.

Discouragement can come calling, like an unwanted suitor, when the next step on our journey seems to be delayed. It normally manifests in the form of questions, such as, "Did I get it wrong? Is this what God really wants? Perhaps I'm not worthy? Why isn't God doing something?"

And if these questions go unanswered, motivation can evaporate into a cloud of impatience, frustration, and even anger.

The thing to do here is keep relating to God, even if that relating may consist, for a time, of mostly presumptuous finger waving at Him. If you've ever read David's Psalms you'll know that God is not easily offended by those who honestly share their thoughts with Him, even when we are wrong. He truly is the loving Father who does not turn away from us even when we are throwing an immature tantrum fuelled by doubt and fear. And in those times, we get to learn the art of settling our spirits to rest in Him and hear His voice again.

Another helpful practice is to return in our thoughts to the last place or time we had a positive outlook about our mission prospects. Remember the wins, the achievements, and milestones along the way to restore faith for the journey.

Our community can help us to not throw in the towel when our mission seems to have stalled. Remember though, that not everyone will "get" your mission, and you don't need them to. It is helpful, though, to have a small but valuable group who do get both you and your mission. Maybe that group is simply you plus one more. Cultivate those relationships that can be the pick-me-up that you need to get back on track, or the wake up call to help you redirect.

The New King James version of the Bible includes the word "suddenly" seventy-five times. That's a reasonable amount I think.

While the natural course of things can sometimes be a gradual build, God will sometimes step onto the pages of your mission story and "suddenly" fling you into orbit!

It can feel like there is nothing...nothing...nothing...still nothing. And then suddenly, acceleration so violently rapid, we think we're going to die. Our protests of "Hurry up, God!" can quickly turn to cowardly shrieks of "Stop the rocket, I want to get off. I wasn't ready!"(If you are getting the idea that I am speaking from personal experience here, you would be right.)

When God launches you, you *are* ready, despite how you may feel.

The Spectacle and the Spectators

I can still remember as a kid, staring wide-eyed at our family's black and white TV screen at grainy footage of men walking on the moon and the spectacular rocket launches. I remember also watching the recovery of returned capsules being plucked from the ocean, and astronauts being helicoptered aboard waiting naval vessels. I think I recall the US President was present for one of them.

I, and a good part of the rest of the world, marvelled at the spectacle of space travel. Of course, it has become so much more common nowadays. I can be outside at night and catch sight of the ISS shining back its reflected light as it passes over head, and barely give it a thought.

But the incredible spectacle of the launch still fascinates us and the promise of reaching beyond and further than has been achieved still thrills. My imagination kicks in today whenever I hear of Mars missions in the planning stages by both NASA and Elon Musk's Space X enterprise.

Depending on your particular mission and the trajectory you will take, you may or may not have any excited onlookers. There may be zero fanfare. And quite likely if your respective national leader was to be informed of your launch and subsequent mission, he or she would probably respond with, "Who? Who's doing what?"

I have a really close friend who I've known for over thirty years. About ten years ago, he was regularly invited to come and speak at various churches and organizations. His personal story is quite incredible and those community leaders recognized the value of hearing my friend's personal story.

Then his trajectory was impacted by a course correction that no one saw coming. About a year into those speaking engagements, he became the sole, full-time caretaker for a family member who is completely incapacitated and uncommunicative. If I tried, I know I would fall well short in trying to describe the sheer intensity of what his life looks like now and how all-consuming his role has become over the past nine years.

In the early years, I secretly feared that my friend wouldn't survive, but I have seen him draw more strength and capacity again and again. I am confounded by him and moved to glorify God for His presence in this man.

Many times, I have caught myself complaining about something in conversation with my friend, only to remember who I am speaking to. I have nothing to complain about! My friend is not only doing what he is doing, but he is doing it with a level of competency that medical professionals applaud. He is very quick to point out his shortcomings and that behind closed doors he is not always a shining beacon of love in service. He admits that he sometimes gets angry and frustrated, but let me say, there is no one I know who conducts themselves with more grace. Honestly, my friend is the greatest example of a human being I have ever met. He is the most Christlike person I have ever known and I feel small if I dare compare myself to him.

Any assistance or respite he receives is incredibly expensive and many times, inadequate. His circumstances have awakened me to the plight of many in our society who are sacrificing themselves in the service of caring for loved ones.

I don't fully understand the purpose of my friend's current trajectory despite spending much time wondering and quizzing God. Sometimes I try to fill in the gaps of my perspective of his journey by dreaming up scenarios that fit my thinking. It doesn't work. God doesn't need my assistance to work it out because He already has it all worked out. I don't fully understand it, but I have come to see value in my friend's life that defies circumstance.

His current trajectory is being lived out in almost complete isolation. Almost no one is aware of what he is doing and the intrinsic value of it, but those current facts have no bearing on the utter importance and value of my friend and his choice to lean into this life course that chose him.

My point is that the significance of your overall mission is not proportionate to how spectacular it appears to others. There isn't necessarily any relationship between others' awareness of and appreciation for your mission, and its actual significance, importance, and ultimate impact. Knowing this will help to keep us from wanting the approval of the crowd, which can derail future progress. If we are looking over our shoulder, waiting for the crowd to show up, we are distracted from the things we need to be doing to keep moving forward.

And let's face it; the crowd's understanding of what is really going on is pretty limited. To illustrate, let us recall any recent news bulletin, where Citizen Joe Onlooker attempts to describe a newsworthy event. Speaking of their recently deceased neighbor the standard response is, "Yeah, he was always very polite and liked to keep to himself." Or this old chestnut, "It sounded like a bomb going off!" used to describe everything from a door slamming, to an earthquake in a neighboring country, to a sonic boom.

Contrast those comments with my earlier quotes from astronauts and you can see the vast difference between the perspective of a spectator and a participant.

It can be nice to have the crowd applauding you, but that is never the goal.

The launch, no matter how public, is never the mission. Launch time, like any other component of our mission cycle, is one step toward mission completion, not the end goal. Astronauts understand this. At the launch, they are definitely in the moment, but they are fully engaged in the moment as a part of the process, propelling them toward their ultimate mission. Jesus did many things on His personal trajectory toward the cross, but He never allowed anything to permanently steal His focus away and He never allowed Himself to be swept along by the crowd, who clearly didn't understand His mission. I can see them on the streets of Jerusalem describing the veil being torn in two (Mark 15:38), "It sounded like a bomb went off!"

Here is another example of how the crowd shouldn't greatly influence us, because it only has a very limited perspective. If you've ever watched a rocket launch, it appears despite all of the power involved, that the vehicle claws its way ever so slowly upward, while spectators remain at a considerable distance from the action for their own safety. The reality is that by the time a shuttle clears the top of the tower it is accelerating through 100 mph (approx 161 kph). That is hardly a dawdle! The distance of the onlookers from the shuttle mean they don't have the understanding of a launch that the astronaut does. Mike Hadfield had this to say of a shuttle launch, "you can truly feel yourself in the centre of it."

The centre of your launch and subsequent trajectory is something you may share with only a few others who share your particular mission. Spectators to your mission only have a limited chance of appreciating, experiencing, or understanding your journey with that same sense of intimacy, and so should have only a diminished level of input into your launch criteria and mission objectives.

The truth is, though, that there actually is another crowd who are cheering us on, like a busload of excited geeks at a shuttle launch. We just don't see them.

Hebrews 12:1-2 tells us:

> *"Therefore we also, since we are surrounded by so great a cloud of witnesses, let us lay aside every weight, and the sin which so easily ensnares us, and let us run with endurance the race that is set before us, looking unto Jesus, the author and finisher of our faith, who for the joy that was set before Him endured the cross, despising the shame, and has sat down at the right hand of the throne of God."*

Be encouraged always. You are not in this alone.

Failure at Launch

I can clearly remember arriving at work early on the morning of January 28th, 1986. Greeting me was the old caretaker who was busily cooking himself some breakfast in between cataloguing his ever-growing Beta home video collection. He kept a portable television on top of the fridge in our lunch room and on arrival I was greeted by the image of the space shuttle Challenger exploding 73 seconds into its flight. I watched it over and over in disbelief. I even went right up close to the screen to try and spot the holes in the story that would surely expose the hoax. But there was no hoax; this was a horrible, almost unbelievable tragedy.

Failures at the launch stage are very rare. The enormous work put in during the planning and training phases virtually eliminate the possibility of failure here. Of course, this assumes that the planning and training was suitable and thoroughly carried out.

In the case of the Challenger disaster, a lengthy investigation took place to identify what went wrong. It identified a design flaw in an O-ring on the SRBs (Solid Rocket Boosters). More scarily was uncovering the cultural failure that created the environment for that physical failure to get to the launch phase.

It was found that NASA was aware of the fault for almost a decade. Yes, you read that right, a decade prior to the accident, NASA managers were aware of the flaw since 1977 (the same year that the first shuttle, Enterprise, took to the air). The investigation highlighted NASA management having poor decision-making processes, violating its own safety rules and on the fateful day, ignoring the warning not to launch.

This truly sad tale serves as a reminder to us of the importance of every stage of our mission process.

The faulty O-rings should have been rectified in the planning stage. The shuttle program formally commenced in 1972 and while it's doubtful that the flaw was recognized that early in the mission cycle, by 1977 the risk was apparent to some at least, but those in authority were not paying attention.

God has already perfectly planned our mission, but within that planning He has made room for our input. There is this mystery that exists between the working of the sovereignty of God and our own freewill. We see it here when He invites us to come into practical alignment with Him and the predestined mission. We cannot sit back and say God has got this, when He is clearly calling us into a cooperative endeavour with Him. When we recognize that something is not right we need to address it. He has given us the powerful capacity to think and the physical ability and strength to take action. These faculties were never meant to lay dormant, but instead to be put to use solving problems and fixing what is within our capacity.

Our ever-watchful Father even prompts us with knowledge and wisdom to act and speak into situations that have a destructive capacity lurking within them.

At the end of the day, NASA did not have a reasonable excuse for its failure, and at the end of the day, neither do we. Remember that God is working in us not only the mission, but a journey toward maturity. Personal responsibility is a part of that expected maturity.

The physical flaw in Challenger was able to persist until the inevitable consequences were finally realized because of the internal flaws in NASA. By then it was too late for the crew of the space shuttle Challenger.

The training phase is that phase essential to identifying and rectifying our own personal and internal flaws. The internal flaws can be most troublesome to identify and the most difficult to rectify, but if left unchecked they can have devastating effects.

Please don't fall into the trap here of shooting for perfection before you start out. We are meant to continue moving forward and addressing issues as they arise. Sometimes they arise as the result of circumstances revealing something hidden inside us and sometimes God will lovingly unveil a hidden obstacle.

Many times He has done this with me, and He continues to do so and normally my response is something like, "Oh man, this sucks. I can't believe that I still have so much stuff to work out. It's not fair that when a problem arises it's always my fault. Thanks, God. What do I do about it?"

The dialogue and the timeframe varies but you get the idea, and once my open ended rant finishes, God begins to speak (or at least I can hear Him again), giving both direction and encouragement.

Flawed decision making could have existed within NASA for many reasons. Likewise, we can have poor decision making. Following are some big-ticket items that can influence the way we make decisions:

Communication

So many difficulties in life, marriage, work, and other relationships can be traced back to poor communication. I touched on this earlier and we can learn better communication skills.

One key is keeping lines of communication open. It can be easy to cut them when difficulty arises. Even more common is to allow them to be blocked by a build-up of unresolved issues that prevent access. Dealing with issues in a timely manner keeps access and communication active (Ephesians 4:26). Think of it like keeping a toxic build-up of plaque from your arteries that transport life giving blood and oxygen around your body. Keep your relational arteries clean so words can bring life and wisdom to each other. This is the foundation from which good joint decisions are made.

Authority

I imagine there is a layered hierarchy of authority at NASA. Interestingly, lines of communication often follow lines of authority.

We have authority relationships and structures in our lives too. They are meant to exist for mutual benefit including the facilitation of the individual and the community to operate with integrity toward their rightful purpose and mission. In practice, this is seldom done well.

Let us consider the theory of 360-degree leadership. The idea of 360-degree leadership is that every individual has a sphere of influence that begins with self-leadership and then extends outward to our peers, downward to those whom we may have authority for, and upward to those who exercise authority over us.

There is great dignity in personal leadership and even more so when it rightly connects with and interacts with the key relationships around us. You can see how this establishes personal responsibility within the context of joint accountability and the right use of authority. Creating this kind of environment establishes effective function, cooperation, communication, and decision making.

If this kind of environment doesn't exist around you, the good news is that you can be the initiator!

Emotion

Our emotions are hugely valuable sensory inputs into all that we do. The danger is when we try to remove them entirely from our framework of reference or when we hand them the steering wheel.

Bottling up or denying our emotions is unrealistic and unproductive, while leading our lives with our emotions as the primary, even the sole, deciding factor in our decision-making process is fraught with danger.

When we can learn to identify why we feel a certain way about a situation we can join that to the other information at hand. This fuller perspective gives us a much better opportunity to make better decisions and experience success.

Am I really suggesting that emotions may have played a role in a shuttle disaster? Consider this: The US defence force, at the time of the Challenger explosion, was viewing the shuttle as a potential platform with defence capabilities. After the disaster, the military opted for the Titan IV rocket over the shuttle. It is possible that anxiety or fear of losing that lucrative contract could have skewed NASA's decision-making capacity.

Challenger had successfully flown nine times previously, alongside four other shuttles in service. Could overconfidence have blinded eyes to the possibility that something could have gone wrong? Remember, some of NASA management had been made aware of the potential for this exact failure.

Christa McAuliffe would have been the first teacher in space. Is it possible that her presence on board Challenger provided pressure to "put on a good show"? America and the world were excitedly watching and NASA knew it. Could that pressure to perform contribute to NASA ignoring the warnings on the day about launch temperatures being outside of the tested launch parameters?

Please understand the inclusion of this dark example here is not to muck rake at NASA's expense. The purpose of identifying mistakes, flaws, and areas requiring improvement, outside of criminal behavior, is not about assigning blame. Identifying shortfalls in either behavior or attitude is simply a part of the process of continual improvement that is required during our lifelong trajectories, toward deliberate mission completion. The person that we are at the beginning of our journey is not yet the person who is capable of mission completion. The necessary qualities and abilities are forged into us along the way, and digging up the flaws is a part of the purposeful process with the end goal being to grow and mature, not merely expose and judge.

Connection with God

Connection with God throughout every phase and scope of life is empowering. Having His involvement in our decision-making process is invaluable. He can bring additional wisdom, larger perspective and even unearth hidden pitfalls that we might otherwise not consider until a potential wrong decision is made. We can tap into His help in making decisions in the same way that we previously discussed in the "Stargazing – Vision" chapter on hearing His voice.

The temptation can be to become so focused on our mission that we become somewhat myopic in recognizing God's input into our co-mission with Him.

Timing

There are many variables that can affect and delay the launch of a space vehicle; weather and mechanical failure being two obvious ones. In a launch of this type there are certain conditions that must be met without exception to launch, some circumstances that need to be within certain parameters and other conditions that on their own may not prevent or delay launch.

There is a range of parameters and conditions that must be met to launch. Mission control doesn't wait for perfect conditions, but safe workable conditions.

We can adopt the same thinking for our personal journeys. If we wait for conditions to be perfect, we may wait a lifetime without ever getting off the ground. If prevailing conditions fit within our criteria we should GO! What criteria? Good question. It obviously depends on you and your unique mission. Outside of that, here are some key indicators:

Peace – Do you have a sense of peace about it?

Circumstance – Is there a workable degree of circumstantial openness and alignment?

Faith – Do you have faith for a positive outcome? (With or without knowing all the detail)

Ignition – Do you know at least what the first step is?

Testimony of others – Do the mature members of your community of people who have an understanding of you and your mission sense green light?

Agreement – Are your travelling companions on the same page?

Authority – Do you have right authorities, who are in agreement?

God's voice – Assuming you have come this far with a sense that this is God's purpose for your life, do you now hear a "No" or a "Wait"?

I recall a well-known pastor that knew he was called by God to start a global Christian movement, beginning in

Sydney, Australia. He came for a season but nothing fell into place so he returned to New Zealand. He didn't go home and despair though. He knew what God had said and came to the conclusion that the mission was right, but he'd jumped the gun on the launch timing. He returned and "take 2" was a very different story, and massively successful…on a global scale!

Often times we can have a very clear sense of the mission, but we can run ahead of God on the timing. In space travel circles this is called "Go Fever". The pressure to get that bird in the air can cause even the most rational and dedicated of people to pull the trigger too soon. Best to get the timing right first up, but even if we muck it up, we can regroup and go again at the right time.

Wrong Mission

When I was a kid I hopped on the wrong bus and realized fairly quickly I was going in the wrong direction. I froze at first and so ended up travelling further in the wrong direction than I needed to. Eventually though, I mustered the courage to ring the bell, get off the bus and cross the street to the bus travelling in the reverse direction back to my starting point.

In adult life, I've found many times for many reasons I've gotten involved in enterprises and activities that have been rather unfruitful, red herrings. Maybe it was out of a wrong sense of loyalty, a selfish pursuit or just misunderstanding God's voice, but either way, after discovering I was travelling in the wrong direction, I was able to eventually course correct. I didn't die, God didn't give up on me, and rather than it being a complete waste of time, God has always taught me something about Himself or myself through it.

He will do the same with you, if you do not quit.

The idea of an astronaut turning up on launch day and trying to access transport to the waiting rocket, if they were not on the designated crew list, is absurd. It would never happen. Security would surely prevent it, but at that stage of a mission cycle, everyone knows which mission they're on and which they're not.

In real life, we can find ourselves on the wrong mission bus. We then have to make a decision to get off. I've seen people ride the wrong mission bus until they are completely disillusioned, lost, and crushed by trying to carry out a mission they were never designed or trained for. I'm not talking about immature, foolhardy individuals. I'm talking about lovers of God who lay down their lives every day in the pursuit of living a life of purpose that glorifies Him.

If you find yourself in this situation, the starting point is to open up honest lines of communication with your fellow travellers and ring that bell to get the driver's attention.

Before we move past launch, let me add in a little disclaimer. When I speak of not doing things that aren't "on mission," for you there is an exception. Actually, there may be many exceptions. When you are a part of a community of any description (family, church, workplace, etc.), there is a necessary responsibility upon the individual to that community. Communities require work for them to continue to function. At home, dishes need to be done; at church, regular meetings need greeters and chairs laid out and coffee makers and toilet cleaners and so on. Workplaces need people who are willing to operate above and beyond their immediate job descriptions to allow the whole team to achieve its goals.

Having a defined sense of purpose and mission is not an excuse to exempt ourselves from day to day responsibilities. No one is too important and no mission is so urgent that we can afford to place ourselves "above" certain responsibilities.

It is never too late to get on God's mission for you. Nothing is wasted. Everything can be redeemed in Christ, the great mission controller.

Launch of the *Trajectory* Book

When we think of the term book launch, our minds likely turn to an event planned to release the book to the public.

In reality there will be three main launches for this book. First, is the launch into writing. It is a very private launch, but the shift from considering the book to beginning the act of writing is definitely a launch.

Second, is the publishing launch. Still largely done behind closed doors (and especially so for online publishing), this launch takes the completed text, formats it, and makes it available to others. I wonder how many completed manuscripts are gathering dust in a drawer or in an archive on a hard drive somewhere. Personally, I have a number of pieces of work that are yet to see the light of day. The temptation is real to never quite finish or to not actually take the next step of publishing your completed work. Publishing your work is a definite and potentially scary next step.

Finally comes the promotional launch where the original book launch picture finds its home.

If publishing is making your work available, then promoting is the act of telling people that it is available. Promoting is essentially saying that this thing I have made has value and is worth people knowing about. It can be an extremely confrontational process, but a very necessary one. The promotional launch for this book will likely be repeated multiple times across different platforms and to different audiences. Such is the sophistication of modern marketing.

The Launch Checklist

1. Do you sometimes get distracted or shut down by fear when it is time for you to take action?

2. Do you have any missions still viable that are waiting to launch?

3. Do you have any final preparations you need to make prior to your next step?

4. If you had to rate yourself for ability to wait and be patient, what score would you give yourself?

5. How could you improve that score?

6. Are you living a life that is about more than just yourself? Relay your answer to a trusted and mature friend.

7. Do you have a sense of the big picture importance of the purposes entwined in your life? Read through the first part of Gideon's story in Judges Chapter 6. How do you relate to Gideon's perspective based on his side of the conversation? What would the angel say to you?

8. Have you ever gotten the timing for something significantly wrong? How can you avoid this in the future?

9. Do you feel like you have ever failed to launch? Are there viable opportunities waiting for you to act on them?

10. What safeguards can you put in place to prevent failures to launch?

TRAJECTORY

11. Do you sometimes feel like you are on the wrong bus? What would it look like for you to ring the bell, get off, and start moving in the right direction?

12. Do you have a healthy appreciation for the opinions of others? How do you weed out what is valid feedback, from what is invalid or unhealthy?

13. Take a few moments to make a list of the things you can enjoy within the unfolding process of your life mission. Thank God for these things.

14. What is God saying to you about the launch chapter?

15. If fear is an obstacle to you taking action, ask for God's help to overcome it and arm yourself with scripture to amplify the voice of faith over fear.

Trajectory – Your Personal Flightpath

The selection and training process for astronauts includes criteria for all aspects of their mission. Each phase of a mission cycle requires different qualities, skills, and strengths. Training and selection therefore includes criteria specific to the flight phase.

The flight phase is a unique, and in some respects unnatural, environment. Arriving immediately after the frenetic pace of the launch, the flight phase shifts pace significantly. This change of pace requires a shift in focus for astronauts and theo-nauts alike.

The Big Slow Down

Our previous quotes from experienced astronauts highlight the massive power and acceleration of the launch. Once achieving orbit the switch off of that power is immediate and speed becomes constant rather than a powerful force mashing you into your seat.

Our forward progress is also marked by times of massive acceleration followed by slower times that can appear like a complete stand still. Just as astronaut's lives cannot be physically sustained indefinitely through massive acceleration, neither can ours. We were not meant to live flat out all the time. In every respect, we function better when we can experience and embrace the different paces that cycle through our lives according to the timing of our individual trajectory.

Just knowing that the pace of life varies helps prepare us for the different seasons and opportune times as they arrive. Knowing can prevent us from thinking when the pace slows that something has gone wrong, that perhaps we have done something wrong. It also helps us to see apparent slow down times as times to recuperate, rest, and reorient ourselves

The astronauts don't panic when the launch phase is over; they immediately begin setting themselves for the flight phase of their mission and the responsibilities at hand.

The Big Silence

Probably the loudest event I've ever attended is drag racing, where the roar off the start line assaults the ears and you better have remembered to bring some earplugs or be prepared to sit there with your fingers in your ears like a complete amateur. The violent noise beats against your chest and shakes everything around you. As impressive as this is, I suspect it falls some way short of the noise of a manned rocket launch.

Astronaut Steve Robinson comments, "It seems the air just isn't big enough for the sound."

That sounds about right.

In her article, "What a space shuttle launch really sounded like", for Universe Today, contributing editor Nancy Atkinson includes a video link to a shuttle launch that attempts to capture the sound of a shuttle at take-off. She goes on to describe the experience at her designated viewpoint almost 6kms away, and the difficulty of trying to capture an undistorted sound recording of such an event. Overwhelming is the word that comes to my mind as I read the various accounts.

All that powerful noise and all the noise of the spectators as they cheer and gasp fades to relative silence as a craft enters orbit.

But truthfully it is not silence. There is one constant throughout all phases of a mission cycle and it seamlessly makes the transition from launch to flight. It is the sound of the constant communication between the astronauts and mission control.

This communication is a constant for life travelers too. Our mission controller, God, is constantly speaking and we have both the opportunity and the necessity to be conversing with Him.

Listening to the dialog between a space flight crew and mission control highlights two things. First, there is the very deliberate nature of the conversation. There is a continual stream of feedback and instruction that is all the time moving the participants forward. The communication ensures that each new task and checkpoint is completed and correct before proceeding to the next, and the next, and so on. Everyone is informed and in no doubt of where they are in the mission cycle, what happens next, and who is responsible for any actions required.

The communication keeps the astronauts moving through the big picture of the mission, by keeping them focused on their current position and the next step. This stays true in normal operation and crisis alike.

Astronauts move toward mission completion by attending to the moment in front of them.

Successful theo-nauts do likewise.

Astronauts move toward mission completion by maintaining clear, two-way communication with mission control.

Ditto for theonauts.
Psalm 119:105 says:

"Your word is a lamp to my feet, and a light to my path."

We can think of this verse in terms of "word" meaning God's written word, but we can equally apply it to His voice speaking today by other means, but always of course, in harmony with His written word.

"A light to my path"—shows that God is able to reveal to us the overview, the bigger picture of our purpose and His vision for our lives, which becomes our joint vision, and the general direction it takes.

"Lamp to my feet"—depicts a more detailed view, revealing the place where we are standing. Think about what it looks like when you hold a torch facing downward to your feet in a darkened setting. It shows up the actual spot where your feet are standing and a smallish pool of light around that spot. It illuminates where you are and just a little bit in front of you. It reveals where you are at and potential next steps.

God's voice in our lives works a lot like this. He speaks from time to time as the "light" in ways that reveal the big picture mission objectives and He constantly speaks as the lamp, orienting us to where we are and a little bit around us. As with the astronauts and mission control conversation, our dialog keeps us moving forward along our mission trajectory.

Our task is to keep our focus mainly on what God is saying in "lamp" conversations, while glancing up at His "light" conversations to confirm we are still moving in the right general direction and make the appropriate course corrections to keep us on that course.

Do we ever make a misstep? The beauty of the constant dialog is that we can very quickly be brought back on course.

When I mistime or misdirect my next step, God doesn't give me the silent treatment (though sometimes, I am tempted to withdraw and shut down on Him). It is at those times I can remind myself that neither mission control nor the astronauts cease communication, because this is the real lifeline for mission and individual.

The second thing that is very noticeable about actual conversations between mission control and flight crew is the personality of the conversation. Yes, it is all very deliberate, especially so at times, but it is not cold or clinical. There is personal connection here.

You can hear in the voices and content that there is relationship here. You can see in the body language of crew as they interact with one another and react to dialog with mission control that there is a knowing of each other. There is of course the necessary professionalism and competency that is conveyed, but it is clearly done with a shared sense of experiencing one another in the mission journey. Looking on, you realize you are seeing real people, with a very outwardly focused objective, relate to one another with a mutual respect and admiration. There is a unity that exists here that fuels the desire for success, and celebrates it every step along the way, because of the personal connection.

This feature of conversation is vital for us to acknowledge and experience in our journey. God is not simply interested in relaying information to us to meet His objectives. He desires to relate to us every step and every moment along the way. In fact, He will have it no other way. We may sometimes get caught up in mission progress, but to God, the relationship formed along the way is as important as the journey itself.

A lifetime mission is cold and hollow, if it does not have loving relationship in it. More on this in our "Mission Debrief".

When I speak of the constant voice of God speaking to us and our ability and need to constantly relate to Him, it is imperative to note that this vertical relationship must be also expressed and experienced on a horizontal plane. Unified, loving, communication and relationship with those who are traveling with us, those who are in our support crew and those to whom we are support to, is as essential to us as it is to the success of our mission objectives.

Relationship within our mission communities is vital to training, inspiration, encouragement, correction, and maintaining perspective of the purpose of our mission (Hebrews 10:24-25). It is through relationship with one another that God continues His work in us to complete us, not just the mission (Proverbs 27:17).

So we've established that the flight phase of a mission cycle, with the constant chatter, is far from silent, though it is considerably quieter than the launch phase.

In an article from the Huffpost, which I reference in the following passages, journalist Dean Praetorius includes a sound bite of the ambient noise aboard the ISS. In the same article, astronaut Chris Hadfield describes the sound as being like "a very large hair dryer." I think most of us can get our heads around this description. Hadfield also informs us that the hair dryer is at its loudest on the ISS, in the toilet. Too much information?

The substantial noise is created by the operating life support systems that are essential to-- you guessed it—the lives of the occupants.

In truth, our lives require maintaining too. The work of maintaining our lives creates some necessary noise that might not being moving us closer to mission completion, but is keeping us functioning through our journey. We all have personal responsibilities that may not be mission focused, but are essential components of the journey. You might consider things in this category that would include family and community responsibilities, the requirement to maintain ones' own health, and as an adult provide financially for ourselves and possibly dependents. These responsibilities can sometimes feel like they are creating ambient life noise that is distracting from our mission. It would be a foolish, and soon dead, astronaut who turned off life support to get some peace and quiet. Likewise, we cannot simply remove ourselves from the noise of life, or try to eliminate the sources of the noise, but we can manage it.

Here too, we can learn from the inhabitants who spend time aboard the ISS. The ISS has a built-in sanctuary. The sleeping quarters are a silent sanctuary among the noise of the functioning ISS. Astronaut Hadfield says the sleep quarters are quiet enough to record music and he ought to know, because he's done it.

While it would be foolhardy for us to try and eliminate genuine requirements and responsibilities from our lives, it is necessary for us to find sanctuary in the midst of it all.

1. Where are the spaces and times of rest in your life?

2. If your life were the ISS, where would your sleeping quarters be?

3. What times, places, and activities allow you to rest and recuperate?

4. What relationships do you invest into that energize you?

Unplugging from the primary purpose is necessary for us to be able to stay the course. The alternative is that we burn out, breakdown, or limp along our journey.

Of course, the ultimate sanctuary is our relationship with God. In knowing Him we can find rest even in the midst of responsibilities and crisis. In knowing Him we see His example of constant rest and zero anxiety as He maintains all of creation. We can and must learn to rest as He does.

In examining the biographies of several astronauts, I notice that many of them have side interests that are totally unrelated to their mission objectives. In their long haul to plan, prepare, and execute their missions, they find the freedom to spend time in non-mission related activities of rest and creativity. We must do likewise. God rested on the seventh day of creation. He does this to show us the freedom to rest during our work cycle.

The Big Nothing

In my final year of high school, 1979, the movie *Alien* was released. It arrived with the tagline, "In space, no one can hear you scream."

Maybe the creator of that line was meaning that in space there is no atmosphere to carry sound waves of any kind, even a scream. Maybe they were highlighting that the distances in space to other people apart from your immediate travel companions are so great that no one is there to hear you scream. I suspect they were cleverly combining both ideas.

Our real-life astronauts experience many changes along the way during their mission. One of those changes is the shift from being surrounded by people to being in almost complete solitude. Up until this point they have been surrounded by teachers, trainers, engineers, support crew, excited crowds, and maybe even adoring fans. In flight, though, they have the company of their mission team in the craft and the thread of communication with mission control on the ground and even some restricted opportunity for social media.

The solitude may come as a welcome relief to some, while others may struggle with it. Remember the selection and training process has already identified potential problems and prepared the astronauts, but it is still an adjustment when it comes to actually experiencing solitude.

You might recall that Jesus was at times surrounded by crowds of people and at other key times He was either completely alone or with the core of His disciples. The crowd came and went by their own will (and sometimes with a little help from the offensive things Jesus had to say to them), but you can see that Jesus deliberately sought out times of solitude and times of greater intimacy with His closest companions.

There is a dynamic that exists in a crowd, but there is opportunity that exists beyond the crowd. Jesus understood His need to be alone and to be alone with the Father. In that space we can enjoy and cultivate that most intimate of relationships with our creator, and reflect and meditate more clearly without the noise and crowd pressing in. Even this takes practice to achieve.

Jesus also created opportunities to share His journey and provide insights to those closest to Him. These opportunities don't exist in the crowd dynamic.

For us to continue to journey forward we need to know when to embrace the crowd dynamic, when to opt for solitude, and where to take time for intimate relationships with those in our inner circles of intimacy.

Our journey will sometimes bring along prevailing circumstances that we must embrace, but we also have the opportunity and the need to create relational light and shade in our personal mission life cycles.

We can, of course, take solitude too far. Actually, we can be quite apt to take most things too far.

Think of an astronaut performing an EVA (Extra Vehicular Activity). Geographically speaking at least, an astronaut alone outside his craft as it traces its course through space is the most alone person in existence. EVAs are undertaken to affect repairs or to carry out the scheduled work for that mission cycle (such as conducting experiments, deploying equipment, etc.).

As we've already discussed, solitude can have a purpose. Solitude outside of an in-flight spacecraft definitely has a purpose. Astronauts enter that unique environment with a purpose, a timeframe and a very specific set of safeguards in place, not the least of which being the self-contained suit (EMU—Extravehicular Mobility Unit), that keeps them alive outside of their normal habitat. They also, always, remain tethered to their craft and have a self-retrieval system (SAFER) if they become detached from the craft.

While it is healthy for us to set aside purposeful alone times, we are never meant to sever our ties to healthy relationships and community.

Astronauts cannot permanently exist outside their craft habitat and there is no reason for them to do so.

We cannot have a healthy existence outside of our natural habitat and there is no purpose that requires it.

In Genesis 2:18 God acknowledges that it is not good for man to be alone. We are made for relationship, intimacy, and community with both God and others.

The Big Joyride

If I were an astronaut, I could see myself making it through all of the phases of my mission preparation to finally be in space and forget about my mission. I'm pretty sure my inner conversation would go something like, "Hey Steve, you've worked hard to get here. You've jumped through all the hoops and ticked all the boxes to get here so why don't you kick back and enjoy it for awhile?"

Can anyone relate?

Reading through accounts from actual astronauts, it is obvious that through their focus on the tasks at hand they do take time to enjoy what they are doing. What they do is in balance with the overall mission, though.

Just getting to the next milestone along our journeys should be celebrated and even savored, but we were never meant to put our feet up and set up camp prior to mission completion.

Can you hear mission control calling out to astronauts aboard the ISS? "Hey guys, we know you're in there. It's time to climb into the Soyuz and come back down. Hello…Hello… come on guys, stop screwing around."

No. The astronauts operate to a timeframe with a designated purpose. Their destination is not to reach the ISS; but to reach it, perform their assigned tasks, and return.

There are plenty of celebrations and obstacles in our flight-path toward mission completion. Forward focus is essential. It requires discipline, but applied discipline results in objectives achieved, and personal growth in terms of character, quality of life, and up-skilling.

Actually, an astronaut's time spent in flight is a fairly intense program of vehicle maintenance, personal care, and task at hand activity that gives them little downtime.

For most of us earthbound travelers, we enjoy much higher levels of discretionary time usage. It can be easy to allow time to slip through our hands. There is a big difference between enjoying the ride and treating life as a joyride.

Self-discipline is one of the hallmarks of those who stay on mission to completion. Some folks seem to have natural reserves of self-control, but it can be cultivated when we realize the importance of our role. Understanding that we have value to add, regardless of circumstance, can become a powerful motivating force to drive us toward success.

We need also to be encouraged that self-control is one of the fruits of the spirit (Galatians 5:22). In God, we are given a capacity to exercise and develop personal discipline.

I can feel my excuses for inactivity evaporating away!

No Pressure!

One of the sneaky little amusements I've discovered in watching internal footage from manned vehicle launches is when you see the astronauts at the moment of experiencing micro gravity. Some astronauts physically react, while it appears that others have been really tensed up and then suddenly relax.

The launch places their bodies under immense physical pressure and within the blink of an eye they are weightless.

But one pressure gives way to another, as it does with theo-nauts. Understanding now that astronauts don't just float around up there on some kind of very expensive, galactic cruise holiday, I'm aware that their transition from launch to flight is an exchange from gravitational pressure to the pressure of managing themselves within an "alien" environment and performing the tasks given them in a timely and correct manner.

In fact, every phase of their mission represents a constant shifting from one set of pressures to another. (Qualifying, learning, training, acquiring skills, teaching, communication, etc.)

We too can expect that during our overall mission cycle we will transition through different seasons requiring different things of us and placing us under various pressures that may be new, but not necessarily be exciting.

Astronauts are trained for every step along the way, but even so, the real-time experience, like the shift to micro gravity, can only be anticipated until it is actually experienced.

Many times, I've suckered myself into thinking, "Yep, this is how things are now," only to have my world turn again to reveal a completely new set of circumstance and challenge

Internal preparation is the key here. Accepting that change comes is the starting point. Knowing that while we may be blindsided, God is not; He is the anchor-point.

Course Corrections

Have you ever wondered how you steer a spacecraft? I have.

As I trawled through material on the subject I came across terms like gimbaling, vernier thrusters, aeronautical flight control surfaces, differential thrust, gravitational assist and "OMS" burn. They lost me when they started talking about Tsiolkovsky's rocket equation and the Hohmann transfer. The Hohmann Transfer, weren't they a band of musicians in the 1970s?

I was feeling quite pleased with myself as I began to read explanations for the above glossary of rocketry. I actually understood some of it. You could explain that away by saying that it's not rocket science, but it actually is! It is clear that writing this book has brought me in touch with my inner nerd. It's ok though, I haven't started wearing sandals with long socks and I've resisted the urge to purchase that deluxe pocket protector off eBay so my pens don't leak on my lab coat.

Reluctantly avoiding some of the technical detail that may not be so fascinating to you, I made some interesting discoveries pertinent to our topic.

There are a number of means of steering a craft during launch, orbit, and beyond. The workings of each aren't critical to this conversation, but what ties them all together is.

Spacecraft, like many other craft, use inertial guidance systems. These systems comprise on-board sensors as input to a central computer which in turn outputs guidance commands to the steering mechanisms. The sensors figure out exactly where the craft is, what direction it is heading in, and how fast it is going. The computer checks that the craft is where it is meant to be at that stage of its journey and then makes any necessary adjustments. Simple!

All of this is happening in real time in a continual loop. This "closed loop" programming means that the computer analyzes input from the sensors against its mission map and makes corrections via the steering mechanisms and then repeats the process again and again for the duration of the mission. By doing this, the guidance system is continually making minute adjustments. If this process wasn't continual, then the craft may go massively off course and either require significant correction or be irretrievable.

There is also an external factor on the spacecraft. Mission control also receives input from the sensors and can make interventional course corrections and adjustments, and can direct astronauts when their input is required as a part of the process.

This is perhaps the most perfect picture I have ever seen of the working together of man and God. That's a big call but let me explain.

Input Sensors

A spacecraft has on-board sensors and so do we. At the most basic level, we have our five physical sensors that give us feedback on ourselves and our surroundings. Smell, taste, touch, hearing, and sight help us move through and interact with the world around us. With these faculties alone we can move toward healthy situations and avoid harmful ones.

We also have our emotions, which provide us some non-physical guidance to the world around us and help us self-analyze. I feel it is important to note here that emotions or feelings are not the steering mechanism, nor are they the controlling computer, but they are a valid and valuable input into the process and when utilized correctly are a major help in navigating our way through life.

If we consider that the purpose of these sensors is to tell us where we are, which direction we are headed in, and how fast we are going, then we must also consider our conscience. The conscience is a built-in moral compass described by the Merriam-Webster dictionary as, "the sense or consciousness of the moral goodness or blameworthiness of one's own conduct, intentions, or character together with a feeling of obligation to do right or be good". It is built into all of us but can be damaged by being overridden. (Acts 24:16, 1 Timothy 4:2)

Our God-born spirit also provides us with feedback that goes above the feedback from our other faculties. Our spirit also, while providing us important positional and directional data, is a significant feature of our central control unit.

The Guidance Computer

From an internal, on-board point of view, our spirit is the central processing unit. Our spirit is the most powerful part of us. Our spirit was designed to be in charge of us. Our spirit has the capacity to position us at exactly where we are meant to be for exactly the right reason and be moving in the perfect direction.

Our mind, operating in our fantastically powerful brains, is meant to operate in conjunction with our spirit to make the decisions and take the actions required for forward progress following the correct trajectory for us. The temptation is to reverse this operational hierarchy and place the brain in ultimate control over the spirit. It is only the human spirit, born from above, that can successfully operate in this primary role. It takes practice. When we persist with a particular thought process we create and reinforce neural pathways and connections that effectively rewire our thinking. When we consistently allow our spirit to take charge of our internal processes and external actions, we strengthen our spiritual muscles for further use.

Mission Control

A space craft and the astronauts aboard do not operate in isolation. There is a very clear understanding that they are on a mission that is bigger than themselves and their decisions and actions must always be taken in conjunction with communication and direction from mission control. Astronauts understand that at times they will need to take the direction of the mission into their own hands and that there are times when mission control assumes complete control. Because they understand the bigger picture requirements and purpose of their mission, they submit to the agreed procedures and protocols and the oversight of mission control. In doing so, the astronauts give themselves the best possible shot at staying alive and of completing the mission at hand.

Here is a clear picture of how we are meant to operate with God throughout our mission. There is a clear purpose and direction that is agreed to. By constant and clear communication throughout the entire life cycle of a mission, the mission objectives are kept in focus as the immediate tasks are completed. There is a beautiful harmony as each member of the mission community knows the scope of their personal responsibility and how it fits into the overall mission context.

I'm not sure about you, but I clearly have a lot to learn when it comes to understanding and correctly operating my internal guidance system. This is a section that I need to read and re-read, so I can put it into practice.

Trajectory of This Book

By the time you read this book it and I will have passed through many stages of our trajectory. The hands-on portion of the journey will largely be over for me as it is picked up by others who will hopefully find it useful for their trajectories.

The scary part of writing is that once the writing is done and the completed work had been handed over to the public, its destiny is largely out of my hands.

What people choose to do with the content can become an intersect with my own mission and flight-path, or just a brief "ships in the night" encounter with no lasting effect.

It takes faith to believe that the writing of this book will be timed to place it into the hands of those who will receive, understand, and apply the message herein.

Trajectory Checklist

1. How do you cope with seasons of different pace along your trajectory?

2. What can you do to remain committed to your purpose, but flexible in your current circumstance?

3. How well do you handle change? Why do you think this is?

4. Do you find it easier to focus on the big picture or on the details?

5. How could you improve your vital communication skills?

6. Consider the way that you use your on-board guidance system. How can you improve?

7. How do you relate to God as your mission controller?

8. How well do you understand your role in your mission?

9. How well do you communicate with and work together with God?

10. How do you cope under pressure?

11. Do you seek solitude or the crowd? Why?

12. Do you have some activities and interests that help you maintain health along your unique trajectory through time and space?

13. Do you have space and time in your life to rest?

14. How do you remain disciplined when there is no external pressure to perform?

15. What is God saying to you about the Trajectory chapter?

16. In your answers above, do you see any areas that you could discuss with Him?

Mission Destination

I found it really difficult to write this chapter, which is the reason I finished the rest of the book and came back to stare at this blank page many times!

First, we all have different trajectories leading us to different destinations with different purposes. You could say that we each have a different destiny, and I don't know what everyone else's destiny is. If truth be told, at times I only have a tenuous grasp on the sense of my own destiny let alone anyone else's. So, I've been questioning what can I write that will be constructive for my readers if I can't speak specifically to your destinations.

Second, the original word and picture that emerged were very much focused on the journey rather than a specific destination. It feels to me that this is an inspired word from my Father in heaven to help us gain perspective and encouragement for our own personal trajectory, by identifying the processes and elements of trajectory in our own lives. If we can recognize those necessary mission components in our lives, we can take a bigger picture approach. We can become responsive rather than reactive in our approach to life and begin to live far more deliberately while maintaining greater peace throughout. You could say that I have felt from the start that the purpose of this book is about helping us mid-trajectory. Of course, we all know that a flight-path is taking us somewhere. That's a given, but we spend most of our time getting there. The name of this book is after all, "Trajectory," not "Destination."

I've written out many prophetic words for individuals but never written a book of a timely message to a wider audience. Throughout the process I've continually asked God to keep me on track. It's important to keep the message His message, without getting in the way. There have been times when the space illustration has become so consuming and fascinating to me that I have had to put my curiosity on pause to prevent me getting "lost in space." It feels like the Father's focus for this message is the journey rather than the destination. Wanting to stay true to that message helped me write myself into a corner.

The other thing I really wanted to avoid is highlighting achievements as our means of worth and identity. We live in a world that measures people by external indicators like achievements, status, wealth, popularity, and so on. It is so easy to do this. I constantly have to correct myself when I start judging a person by what I can see with my limited perspective. Similarly, I can find myself doing a stock-take of my own life to determine my current identity and worth.

Our identity and value aren't derived from these things. It is when we allow the world around us to shape our conclusions about who we are, that we are in real danger of coming up with the wrong answer. It is only when we gaze at God long enough that we begin to see ourselves as His reflected glory. It is then we can join the psalmist and say, "I am fearfully and wonderfully made." It is then that we gain a true appreciation that who we really are is not dependent on our surrounds.

It may have been an unreasonable fear to associate too much talk about destination with fuelling our love of achievement-based assessment of ourselves and others, but it is a fear I had to work through in the process of writing.

I could also feel my own perspectives shaping my reluctance to write this chapter. Cast your mind back to the Jews' journey out of the wilderness and into the Promised Land. It is pretty clear to see the trajectory of a nation moving from impoverished slavery to abundant living in communion with their God.

Over the years, my personal view of these passages has shifted from the "destination" of the Promised Land to the steps taken; the "Trajectory." Where I have begun to find most value in this epic illustration is in the circumstances along the way. The picture that has emerged to me is the work of God in the lives of His people. He quite deliberately uses the circumstances they faced to reposition their hearts. With each hurdle and even each failure, God is giving His people opportunity to purify their hearts and relate more intimately with Him. The same is true for us. Hence my willingness to eagerly write about our overall trajectory, while being less concerned with a destination. Destination is important, but God's concern is for the state of our heart and our relationship with Him as we journey and arrive.

The whole truth is that for the Jews there was a destination. The whole truth for us too is that while the journey is important, we are moving toward a destination.

I couldn't see how to convey this until I had a meandering conversation with my wife, where as usual we conversationally solved all of the problems of the world. You know the kind of conversations that normally start in the shallows and gradually move out into deeper waters without any particular agenda. The kind of conversations where you find yourself saying stuff that is absolutely true, but you weren't aware that you knew it. In fact, you didn't know it until that moment. I'm so grateful to God for giving me a wife who is passionate about Him and who indulges my waffling, waiting for a nugget of truth to emerge. Sometimes the wait is longer than others!

The conclusion that we arrived at is that I should share with you a slice of my own trajectory with a glimpse of our projected destination.

A Modern-Day Love Story

The niche I'd like to focus on is our marriage so let me start with a little tour down memory lane.

Vicky and I were raised on opposite sides of Australia, and it was a working holiday when I was about nineteen that brought me into her neighborhood. We came from similar backgrounds, growing up in families that would be considered middle class. Two of the struggles we each identified with in our families of origin were alcohol and finances.

When we met, we were both pretty immature, aimless, poorly equipped for life, and with a really low sense of self-worth. Honestly, what could go wrong? We started dating and moved in together, and as you might expect after a while our relationship began to self-destruct.

You know I tell people that we started out as a clueless couple and they smile and nod with understanding, but seriously, we were clueless! Trying to make decisions was like pulling teeth. Trying to communicate when it really mattered? Don't even go there. We poorly managed ourselves, were socially dependent on alcohol and without direction. It was a recipe for disaster, and by the time Christ came to our rescue we were really just staying together out of convenience.

Christ did come to our rescue though, when we weren't even looking for Him. His presence in our lives brought fresh perspective for everything.

One of the first things we did was to move to separate bedrooms. We would go to bed and talk to each other through the wall at night. We didn't give it a lot of thought at the time.

We weren't trying to meet some legal requirement of being a Christian, we just wanted to honour God and we thought this was a good start. Looking back now, I think that simple decision tickled His heart so much that it is one of the reasons why we enjoy such favor on our marriage today.

Our thoughts began to turn to the future, with questions like, "does God want us to be together for life?" He made it very clear that the answer was yes. I made a plan to ask Vicky to marry me and then blurted out my request prematurely. It seems I couldn't wait and it felt like neither could God.

We had gone to the movies to see *Romancing the Stone* but it was sold out, so we decided to see *The Temple of Doom*. Fortunately, this wasn't an omen for our marriage! While we were waiting out the shift in session times the question just popped out. It was like an involuntary action. I was just as surprised as Vicky! Her answer thankfully was "Yes." I am not disappointed at all, but looking back it feels like I was moved by God's loving eagerness for the two of us to be together as husband and wife.

Some months later we were married and a redeemed relationship chapter began. Our journey has been dotted with a few surprises along the way, but for the most part our growth as individuals has come slowly and sometimes with great pain.

Like most marriages, ours has at times been a bumpy ride. Circumstances beyond our control and our own shortcomings have contributed to seasons of turbulence, but have also been used to positively shape us and redirect our course.

In more recent years we began to notice people noticing us. People often pass comment about the way we relate to one another and strangers often assume that we are newlyweds, still enjoying the honeymoon phase of our marriage. Not a bad result considering we have been married for thirty-three years and counting.

Slowly it began to dawn on us that we had a story worth telling. It has become crystal clear that stored up in the message of our love story is hope for others. Becoming aware of this has helped us to identify what works for us and become very deliberate about communicating that to others. As a result, we have begun to develop marriage resources and make ourselves available to couples who want to build into their relationships.

I share this snippet of our story here to let you see a small portion of our personal trajectory and acknowledge the degree to which we have begun to live in our destination. It is not the complete picture, but in sharing it I hope you will begin to see that God had a vision for our lives before we even were a "we." He had a plan to lead us toward His vision, revealing it to us as we were ready to accept it, and to train us and prepare us in the areas where we needed to grow. I hope also that you will recognize His presence in our journey, every step along the way, and believe that He is waiting for us in what is as yet unfulfilled.

Your destination is one of purpose. You were designed and created in loving purpose. Your life, every element of it, is being purposefully fit together to move you forward and into a destiny with eternal value. Your eternal value is not dependent on your destination. Your personal value and the magnificence of your true identity are never up for grabs, because of who created you. God doesn't do counterfeits and He doesn't make rubbish. You are highly prized by Him.

So Many Destinations, so Many Purposes

Getting back to our space analogy, let's consider some of the many space programs completed, in progress and planned.

Early space flight quickly became focused on getting men to the moon and back. Each mission was a learning exercise to confirm what was already known and within reach, and to take the next logical step to fulfil the vision of getting to the moon.

Like those early missions, others have gone before us and made discoveries that we can build upon. We are lifted by the legacy of others' lives lived well. We benefit from the example of those who stayed the course and completed their mission, reaching their personal destination. We also have the opportunity to leave a legacy for others.

The Voyager program launched the probes Voyager 1 and Voyager 2 in 1977 on their grand tour of the outer planets of our solar system. Not only have both craft completed their missions, they have continued to journey and function far beyond their originally intended purpose. One day in the not too distant future their power units will run down to the point where they will continue to hurtle through space without the ability to read their surroundings or communicate back to Earth. They will effectively die.

In the meantime, they have sent back a wealth of information and new discoveries. Their trajectory was carefully planned to use the forces of their surrounds to propel them onwards to their destination of discovery and communication of a finite set of data. They have reached their destination but have not arrived. They had a purpose that was greater than anyone could have anticipated.

Every time I try to lock in my destination and purpose, God reveals a little more to me. The same will be true for you. We hit targets and rendezvous points along the way and think we have made it only to find that God peels the curtain back a little further to allow us to see more of what He sees.

These craft had the purpose of discovering new information along their unique pathways and communicating it back to Earth. Our purpose, in general, is to make discoveries along our trajectories and meaningfully communicate to others. Our purpose is to reveal heavenly truths to those around us so they might follow our legacy.

These craft had significant encounters and destinations along the way. We will likely have significant encounters and circumstances along our way that will serve to redirect and propel us along the right course, building a progressively revealed and experienced destination that fulfils us, glorifies God, and reveals truth to others.

Closer to home, the ISS is home to a constant rotation of experiments. Discoveries from these experiments give us new technologies and information that eventually filter their way into modern life. Hopefully, discoveries made will be put to use for positive outcomes. Of course, the destination of discoveries made is at the discretion of those who own the information. They get to dictate how it is used and who benefits from it.

Each of us has a unique pathway providing different perspectives and opportunities to make discoveries. We always have a choice of what we do with the findings from our journey and how we communicate to others. In communion with God there is a responsibility to honor and serve Him with our experiences and findings, but we can use our will in selfish pursuits.

The Cassini craft has recently (2017) been in the media again, as the mission came to a fiery end.

The craft launched in 1997 as a part of the joint Cassini-Huygens mission. The Cassini craft explored Saturn and its rings from orbit while the Huygens craft landed on Saturn's largest moon, Titan. The launch date was in 1997, but the vision for the mission and planning commenced way back in 1982.

This was a mission with shared purposes, employing multiple craft, and planned and executed by cooperative international space agencies.

What a great example of partnering together in a unified fashion to achieve complimentary purposes and reach multiple target destinations. Our potential to achieve is multiplied when we appropriately cooperate with each other and operate with unity. Our own success can be made more certain when helping others to achieve their purposes and reach their destinations.

Like the Voyager missions, Cassini, having reached its destination, had its mission life extended and re-extended as it continued to outlive its originally intended mission life. As far as missions go, Cassini massively over-delivered.

The decision to destroy Cassini was taken to eliminate the possibility of it crashing into a potentially habitable moon of Saturn and contaminating it. Its life was planned down to the last second and Cassini's grand finale was a carefully orchestrated set of manoeuvres, picking up a redirect from the moon Titan, and threading between the rings around Saturn itself.

Our lives mimic Cassini in that we have value and purpose down to the last moment and the smallest detail. We need to remember that. Maybe it is a stretch too far, but I can't help but think of Christ. The final act of Cassini's Earth-connected existence was to protect a possibility of life. Christ gave His life for an even greater cause, that all might know abundant life eternal.

Years beyond Cassini's mission, data received will be unpacked and will potentially benefit mankind. Jesus' sacrifice on the cross goes on benefitting all who will receive it, millennia after His incredible sacrifice, and will continue to do so for the rest of this age.

Our lives, when traveled well, may end in many ways, but to the end we have the opportunity to leave a powerful, living legacy to future generations.

Ultimately, our destination is eternity in God's Kingdom and we are meant to be living there now, even while constrained to our earthly existence.

In the not too distant future a manned mission to Mars will take place. It has been in planning for some time and is some way off our ability to achieve just yet. Even then, the planned mission is a one-way ticket. While there is a theoretical possibility to return a craft from Mars using an orbital kick-start from Mars, current NASA plans are to establish a camp on Mars where the transplanted inhabitants will live out their lives.

Like most of our space travel so far, planned Mars expeditions are missions of exploration and discovery. The costs will be high in every respect, but the results will be learned from and built upon by others.

I can imagine that our eventual space travel will include recreation and productive activities most likely in the pursuit of resources and energy. What is theoretical science or even science fiction today will one day likely be commonplace.

Our lives can have massive impact on the future of others. The scale and scope of our influence and achievement has less to do with how good we are, and more to do with how God has individually wired us and the specific plan and destination He has for us(Romans 12:3-6). Our job is to discover our journey, our purpose, and our destination in relationship with Him, and then go live it out, doing what we can and growing in trusting in Him through it all.

Destination of the Trajectory Book

This book will have many milestones in its life. Completion of writing the originally inspired idea, publishing the final work, and then giving it a profile in the marketplace through promotion and even achieving sales targets are examples of some milestones.

None of those things though, is the ultimate destination of the book. The book will of course arrive at physical and digital destinations, but these aren't what I would consider to be the true destination of this book.

The true destination of this book is when it arrives in the heart of its readers and begins to be lived out. I will never be able to fully appreciate how well it arrived at the desired destination, because that will be beyond my capacity and because the destination will be a progressively experienced one.

I will not have a full understanding of the destination, but God will. Perhaps in eternity He will share it with me.

Mission Destination Checklist

1. Reread "A Modern Love Story" and try and identify the different components and stages of our trajectory.

2. Think about an area of your life in terms of your trajectory. Can you identify some of the significant phases and elements? Can you begin to see a destination? Can you see how you may have partially at least begun to live in your destination?

3. Thinking about your personal trajectory and destination, attempt to write out a description that you could communicate to others as I have done with my modern-day love story.

4. Ask God to help you have a perspective on who you are and why you are. Try and write it down. If you're not sure where to start find what scripture says about you as a created child of God.

5. What is God saying to you through this chapter?

6. I listed a number of actual space missions. Each one had clearly defined purposes and objectives (destinations). Some shared physical destinations and even built upon the findings and results of previous missions. How can you better celebrate and learn from the missions of others? Whose lives are you building your life mission upon?

7. Can you sum up your main purpose in one sentence?

8. Referring to the previous question, repeat the process for additional purposes you see in God's plan for your life.

Mission Debrief

Thinking about hurling an object that weighs not too far short of 200 tons into space, to a velocity of around 17,500 mph is mind boggling. The sheer power required to achieve such a feat is enormous. We've already talked about the noise associated with a launch, but the accompanying visual spectacle is, well, it's spectacular.

Understandably, the majority of the weight of a launch vehicle is fuel. That's right, most of the bulk of a launch vehicle is completely utilized and expended in lift-off.

There is a power at work in the lives of those who choose a life of purpose. It is a power that reveals the course ahead, the mission objectives, and propels the theo-naut along his or her unique trajectory. It is a power far greater than that required to launch a vehicle into space. It is "Love."

The greatest power in the universe is love. Love is the substance that binds creation together. Love is the purest reflection of our Father in heaven's nature. Love is what does not quit or fail. Love is the ultimate renewable energy source.

Love is the "Why" and the "How"

If you've taken part in exploring a vision and setting goals toward that vision, you may have come across the notion that,

"If your why is big enough," you will do what is required to achieve your goals. It is true. If your motivation, your why, is great enough you can persist through to success, no matter what obstacles and challenges you face.

As a component of our marriage coaching, my wife Vicky and I include goal setting. In recent times, we've started to include the advice for couples to set goals and develop a forward vision for their lives that are driven by love. Doing this is a built-in failsafe for everything you set out to achieve. Begin in love, continue in love, and finish in love.

Remember that "love never fails." (1 Corinthians 13:8)

It's only three words but it is a big truth. It's a let's do something we've never done before kind of truth. It's a never give up kind of truth. It's a powerful kind of truth.

Love doesn't quit, love doesn't come to an end, love achieves what it sets out to do, and love propels and lifts.

People quit and fail, I have sometimes quit and failed, but when we choose to love, we find a way.

I remember a situation a couple of years ago where I had definitely moved out of love. It was a situation that turned from bad to worse despite God's instruction to me to love. I mean God wasn't even subtle about it. I would approach this situation on a daily basis, almost dragging myself to face it. The dark cloud that hung over my thoughts felt like it was actually visible to those around me. God spoke to me directly, through counsel from others, and He even placed signposts in my path to seize my attention. There was a time when every morning I would start the day with the Huey Lewis and the News song, "The Power of Love" playing somewhere within earshot. What a coincidence. Come on! Sometimes I'd "try" to love, but in reality, I wasn't paying attention, and of course the situation fell apart and whatever opportunity there might have been was lost.

Interestingly enough, a similar situation arose recently. I saw it developing and immediately thought, "Ok, God, I can see what's happening here. You are giving me another opportunity to love better. You are taking me around the mountain again so I can increase my capacity to love, because that is what this situation and these people need."

I'd love to say that I aced it and lives were changed, but the jury is still out. I have definitely improved my capacity to love, but I have a way to go. I suspect God will bring more opportunities my way to continue to work on my love muscles.

Have you ever noticed that opportunities sometimes do repeat themselves to provide more practice for our weakness? Consider how God led Israel through the wilderness after their failure. That going around in the wilderness would eventually result in timely propulsion into their promises.

Free Love, Man!

In space travel beyond earth orbit, the planning phase of a mission includes calculating the use of heavenly bodies to provide "Free Travel."

Currently, vehicles launching from Earth use most of their fuel and mass just to reach orbit, leaving little fuel to travel anywhere else. Vehicles then need to use "gravity assist." Essentially the space craft uses the gravitational pull of the planet or moon it is near to, to potentially change its direction and velocity.

This way spacecraft can make relatively small, timed inputs of thrust that position them to take advantage of free propulsion far more powerful than their own capacity.

In this way, generations of space missions from lunar missions, to the more recent Cassini mission, to proposed Mars missions, have traveled farther for very little fuel input.

I can't help but be reminded by this technique of "gravity assist," of the operational power of love in our lives.

Each of us has the capacity to achieve certain things within the constraints of our natural abilities.

But it is when we choose to align ourselves with God that we receive a heavenly assist. By expending relatively small amounts of love to position ourselves near God, we receive a disproportionate amount of "push" and redirection from Him.

When we choose love, we are choosing to operate with the Kingdom of Heaven's currency. When we choose love, we no longer are restricted to operating out of our own fuel tank. We begin operating from God's capacity of love. When we choose love as our "why" and our "how," we are energized, redirected, and propelled forward.

There are many experimental propulsion systems in development right now. It is possible that at some point in our future we may be able to travel much greater distances at much greater speed, and without the need to time that travel schedule to pick up the push from heavenly bodies. What will remain true though is that future space voyagers will not be doing so with a power that is their own. Astronauts and theo-nauts alike will always be dependent on a greater power. For theo-nauts that power is love. We do have a capacity for love and when we join it with the power of our heavenly Father's love, it is an unstoppable force.

Can I encourage you to take a moment and consider this passage? It is so vital for us to understand the vast power of love available to those who will align themselves with God. It is a power that can raise a man, or a plan, from the dead. It is a power beyond comprehension, but not beyond reach.

What Does Love Look Like

Take a step back and think again about the phases of a mission cycle. There are countless opportunities along the way to quit or fail on both a personal level as well as the big picture stuff. What about your progress so far along your mission trajectory? You may never have thought of your life in these terms. The whole illustration of this book is simply to get us to think about our lives in a deliberate and purposeful way.

What does love look like for us, though? The greatest, most condensed, set of instructions for love is 1 Corinthians 13 as a whole. Vicky and I catalog the contents of this chapter with our marriage coaching clients.

If 1 Corinthians 13 is the condensed version of how to love, then perhaps John 15 is the pocket guide to how to love God.

If you want to measure your progress at love, hold your behaviour and attitudes up against the light of these passages and the example shown us by Jesus. If it is uncomfortable to do, know that you are not alone.

Your Love, Your Mission

When the mission objectives are clear and valued, the mission will endure through whatever difficulties arise. Forward progress may sometimes falter as the next solution is being unearthed, but until someone calls it quits it is still game on!

Now think about your mission cycle. Think about your trajectory and the difficulties you've encountered. Think about the times when love has been thrown out the window.

Jesus committed the greatest act of love at the cross. He endured it because of the joy that was set before Him (Hebrews 12:2-3). It is the greatest act of love made possible by the greatest source of love (John 3:16). That same love is available to us both to receive and express as children born in the likeness of our Father.

Jesus' motivation was love, both for the Father and for us. That love showed up as unwavering obedience to the Father, single-mindedness in His journey to the cross, and the ultimate sacrifice of His innocent life on the cross.

When love is the fuel for our journey we will stay on course to mission completion and when our trajectory takes a course that we were not expecting, we rest in the knowledge that the Father knows what is going on. The Father also knows our capacity (1 Corinthians 10:13).

Your Non-sequential Trajectory

For the purposes of writing this book, I've presented the phases of the mission journey in a sequence that most logically represents a mission cycle. The reality for the theo-naut is that the process of progress along our unique trajectory is actually not sequential.

While it makes sense to try and order the elements of this book into a sequential timeline, you are probably already aware that life is never as clean cut as that. In reality, the living out of our mission cycle sees us revisit all of the phases of mission many times.

We revisit the stargazing phase as we gain a bigger, clearer perspective with some progress in the other phases. We don't have the capacity to hold a vision for the whole journey from the start. As we grow into the mission by executing the mission, the mission executes growth in us. That growth increases our capacity to see further ahead.

It is also as we proceed along our mission timeline with God that our relationship deepens and He is able to share larger perspectives, and He allows us to sense the motivating desire in His heart for our journey. We become more intimately engaged with both God and the mission.

The planning phase is an ongoing work as we spend our lives with God bringing us up to speed with what He has already planned, and getting our heads around the role that we play in that plan. As we looked at earlier, just when we think we have everything nailed down, the wind blows and we find ourselves re-calculating again.

What can I say about the training phase? Basically, we never leave. When it comes to training, we are always in need of more. We never get to the stage where we can honestly say, "Yep, I am the complete unit, I am across every detail of my trajectory and it is all completely within my capacity." But you already knew that. Every time I have been tempted to think along those lines even in one small slice of life, opportunity soon arrives to reveal to me the sobering truth that there is another level to be tapped into. I am always in need of growth, and so are you.

The launch phase is also repeated as you reach new milestones along your journey, moving into new seasons of your timeline. Sometimes the transitions are only noticed in hindsight. Other occasions are as spectacular, scary, and exciting as a real-life rocket launch.

Your trajectory phase is not just a trajectory phase. In a space mission the stages are clearly defined and after launch, the vehicle follows a trajectory to complete its mission.

For theo-nauts, the trajectory includes every phase. Your trajectory is all of the elements together. Your trajectory is your complete timeline, not just the part where it feels like you are executing your mission.

Knowing this helps us to appreciate every step along the way. The temptation when we are enduring a particularly difficult season is to just wish it was over. Knowing that we have a purpose can actually cause us to rush the process. We can pressure ourselves into trying to close out each phase to get to the next one.

Closing Notes

Throughout the course of my life I've been fortunate enough to rub shoulders with some amazing people whose lives are an inspiration to all, present company included. Some of those people have been very visible in the public arena and others have been hidden away as they live out their life's purpose.

For all of them I am incredibly grateful for the richness they have brought into my life, and I'm grateful to my Father in heaven also, for each of those relationships.

I started off this book by recounting a conversation with a mate where the word "Trajectory" came to mind. If you can remember that far back, this setting was the seed from which this book grew.

That mate was Brett Higgins. I only met Brett and his amazing wife Susie earlier this year (2017), so I haven't known them for a large "quantity" of time, but it has been a large "quality" of time.

It's interesting that God would highlight the word trajectory to me when speaking to Brett, because he and Susie, "Team Higgins," are already a great example of two people living out their God given trajectory toward His ultimate mission for their lives.

Team Higgins, to me, are the poster children of the idea of trajectory. And when I say the idea, I mean the actually living out of that idea. There is a dignity and nobleness in them that commands respect and yet there is humility. They have incredible vision matched with the discipline to draw that vision into reality. They are undoubtedly connected with God, but without loss of the wonderful humanness that makes them all the more relatable and likable. They are true theo-nauts.

It is clear that Team Higgins have a long and exciting trajectory ahead of them, some of which still remains unclear to them. Like them, I can't wait to see what it will look like.

When I was a child my dad would set off fireworks in our backyard on that one night of the year that it was allowed. The excitement was palpable. We would fidget impatiently as Dad nailed the spinning wheels to the fence and placed the larger rockets in bottles, semi-steady, for launch.

Once the fireworks started we were transported to a land of wonder and awe. Our heads leaned back and our eyes swivelled upward, riding each soaring stream of fire and sparks to its destination in the sky far above us. Each projectile exploded in a magnificent shower of sound, warmth and light. Our upturned faces flickered in the magnificent display of controlled chaos and involuntary "Oohs" and "Aahs" escaped from our mouths.

Once the final rocket had left its beer bottle launch pad, mum would hand out sparklers so my sisters, brother, and I could take our part in the proceedings. We would run around the yard in a somewhat loony fashion, fueled by the excitement and perhaps a little bit of fear at holding this spitting, hissing stick in our hands.

For a small boy, the excitement was off the charts, but I remember thinking that one day it would be my turn to set off the fireworks!

On the odd occasion that I get to see fireworks nowadays, there is still a sense of wonder. As I look around me at those times, I can see that it is a shared sense of wonder. Not all of the skyward grins and exclamations are from the children.

Team Higgins, and people like them, remind me of those fireworks. They are tracing a magnificent trajectory through their allotted time and space and taking their part in a magnificent display. They are people who cause me to lift my eyes up and embrace a sense of wonder.

I want to live a life that inspires wonder in others.

I want to live a life that causes others to look up.

I want to live a life that causes others to know that they have fireworks to set off.

I want to live a life that causes my maker to say "Wow!"

I want to live a life that causes others to honor my maker.

How about you?

Mission Debriefing: The Trajectory Book

As I already mentioned, I can't accurately evaluate the effectiveness of *Trajectory* hitting its mark and fulfilling the intended mission. I can however share with you the effect of the mission on me.

This is a perfect example of how God is not just using me to fulfil a mission but He is working in me to achieve His mission. I did not set out at all to be personally affected by this project, but I have been.

Along the way there has been a real sense of working together with God to share something on His heart. Honestly, at times it has felt like He has been dictating to me the words coming to the page. Can you imagine what that feels like? Actually, I hope you don't have to imagine. I hope that if not already, you will soon experience the sheer privilege and joy of being on co-mission with Him.

About two years ago I felt God challenging me as a father would challenge His son, to begin to experiment with the prophetic. So far, I have only just stuck my toe in the water, but writing *Trajectory* with the notion that it has a prophetic origin and message feels a lot bigger than "one small step for man…"

Fear and doubt would say, "what if it isn't inspired by God" or "what if it was but I got off track?" What if? You get to be the judge!

Along the way, God taught me so many things that I didn't know I didn't know. Searching through scripture and taking the time to think about things will do that to you.

I have had to apply trust throughout the process and will continue to need to do so as this book enters the market. I have to trust that He will put it into the hands of those whom He has intended it for. Fortunately, I can discuss all of this with Him and ask Him for His input and intervention.

I've experienced what it was like to get really stuck at one stage, to the point that the book only became unstuck with help from someone else. It was a great honor to have my wife come to my assistance and to be able to work together in this way. Here was further evidence of another valuable lesson for me.

I got to exercise discipline in aiming for my original deadline. I got to exercise more discipline when I missed my target and had to push on to completion anyway. Do I need to develop greater discipline? You bet I do!

One of the superficial kicks I got out of writing *Trajectory* was that I had the opportunity to delve a little deeper into a subject that interests me. I don't consider myself a space nerd, but others might! From time to time I hear titbits of news about what's happening in space that piques my curiosity, but it's not something I find the time to pursue. Writing this book has allowed me to dive in, following lines of thought into some fascinating space related subjects. I have had to restrain my conversations, when I see someone's eyes glaze over I stop talking.

Anyway, I hope that you can see that this particular mission of writing has had a harmonious combination of personal impact and blessing entwined with benefits and purpose beyond myself, in the lives of others and contributing to my relationship with the Father.

While the details of this particular mission are mission specific, the balance of benefits are not. The combination of mutual blessing of God, others, and self enroute to your life of purpose are key indicators that you are on track. I have a flawed tendency to think in terms of either/or. This thinking plays things like outcomes off against one another. God is bigger than that. The God who came to give us abundant life (John 10:10), says that we can live lives that meet three criteria. God is able to find pleasure in us, while being our delight as we serve others.

Your trajectory toward your life mission is meant to be characterised by the growing love relationship between us and the Father, and an abundance in our lives that is deliberately spilled over into the lives of others. This is not a commandment, but rather a statement of hope that we can aspire to.

If you take a snapshot of any given day in our lives it may not feel true, but if we continually allow God to enlarge our perspective, we will begin to see it and experience it more and more.

Mission Debriefing Checklist

1. Spend a couple of minutes thinking about the verse, "Love never fails." What is the meaning of these words, applied to your life?

2. If love is the "why" of your life mission, express your mission in terms of love.

3. If love is the "how" of your life mission, what will it look like for you to remain in love?

4. What acts of love can you make to position yourself nearer to the Father and in place to take advantage of the powerful propelling force of love?

5. How do you show love to others, from those closest to you to strangers?

6. What thoughts and attitudes are you holding on to that may be taking up precious space that could be occupied by love?

7. Can you identify some big, uninvited circumstances in your life that have or could propel you in the right direction with greater power? Thank God for them.

8. 1 John 4:16 includes the statement, "God is love." What is the impact of this truth on your life and identity, remembering that we are made in His likeness and have His spirit in us?

9. How do you show love to God?

10. What is God saying to you from the mission debrief chapter?

11. Pray about God's message for you in this book.

12. Pray over your responses to the checklists. Revisit them and invite His direction and redirection.

May your life from this day forward be a blast!

Notes

Introduction

Merriam Webster's Collegiate dictionary (Eleventh edition)
Definition of "Trajectory"

Business Insider
https://www.businessinsider.com.au/canadian-chis-hadfield-describes-a-shuttle-launch-2012-12#sjw0KS9j3x-KHpTve.99

Stargazing

Wikipedia
https://en.wikipedia.org/wiki/Timeline_of_the_Space_Race

Planning

Smithsonian National Air and Space Museum
https://airandspace.si.edu/multimedia-gallery/5317hjpg?id=5317

NASA
wall chart of the process flow for a NASA project/Program

Lance Walnau
https://lancewallnau.com/

Short Circuit **(movie)**
https://www.youtube.com/watch?v=RBtRVjAMbVo

Hidden Figures **(movie)**
https://www.youtube.com/watch?v=RK8xHq6dfAo

Training

The Kennedy Space Center
https://www.kennedyspacecenter.com/

The Right Stuff **(movie)**
https://www.youtube.com/watch?v=ElzIPn1pXWE

Launch

howwelivestories.com
https://howwelivestories.com/2011/07/08/so-astronaut-mike-good-whats-it-like-to-go-into-space/

Daniel Pink
http://www.danpink.com/

Mike Hadfield singing David Bowie's "Space Oddity"
https://www.youtube.com/watch?v=poZCINzxzrQ

The Rogers report
(Report of the PRESIDENTIAL COMMISSION on the Space Shuttle Challenger Accident)

https://history.nasa.gov/rogersrep/v1ch4.htm

Trajectory

Nancy Atkinson writing for Universe Today
https://www.universetoday.com/94919/
what-a-space-shuttle-launch-really-sounded-like/

Shuttle launch video with audio
https://www.youtube.com/watch?v=OnoNITE-CLc&feature=youtu.be

Dean Praetorious writing for Huffpost (Sound onboard the ISS)
https://www.youtube.com/watch?v=OnoNITE-CLc&feature=youtu.be

Merriam Webster's Collegiate dictionary (Eleventh edition)
Definition of "Conscience"

General

You can find a wealth of information at the NASA website, as I did. I even downloaded the astronaut candidate application form while I was there, but I don't think any of my work colleagues were overly convinced when I left it conspicuously laying on my desk at work!

NASA
https://www.nasa.gov/

The Rocket Boys and October Sky

The "Rocket Boys" book authored by Homer Hickman is a great true story read about a boy who grew up to be a key player at NASA. It's a neat read, but if you prefer, the movie inspired by the book, "October Sky" is really well done too.

The Bible
My biggest reference book for this "Trajectory" book has been the Bible. It has also been the biggest reference book for my personal trajectory. I have deliberately listed it last here because it is the foundation which all other knowledge and wisdom rests upon. My weapon of choice is currently the "New King James" version. If you're not familiar with the text, allow me to suggest getting hold of either a hard copy or digital version. If you're not sure where to start, ask someone who might know. If you don't have someone who might know, send me an email and I'll try to help you get started.

steven@enthusiasticmarriage.com

About the Author

When he is not writing, Steven and his wife Vicky are marriage coaches, (see enthusiasticmarriage.com). They live in the beautiful city of Perth in Western Australia, close to their adult children and new granddaughter.

The coaching came partly as a result of the success of Steven's first book, *A Simple Plan – How to Have the Marriage of Your Dreams*, which reached top ten bestseller status in its category on Amazon. Steven has enjoyed a long career working in the automotive and mining industries, requiring a high degree of mechanical aptitude. This background has geared this author's writing to identifying and communicating practical solutions.

His personal relationship with God also sees Steven bring a perspective of deliberately partnering together with God to do life well.

Trajectory is an inspired book that picks up on the purposeful living theme that Vicky and Steven share with their clients, and are progressively seeing realized in their own lives.

www.ingramcontent.com/pod-product-compliance
Lightning Source LLC
Chambersburg PA
CBHW061330040426
42444CB00011B/2846